Clear Speech

Pronunciation and Listening Comprehension in North American English

Second Edition

Student's Book

Judy B. Gilbert

CAMBRIDGE
UNIVERSITY PRESS

PUBLISHED BY THE PRESS SYNDICATE OF THE UNIVERSITY OF CAMBRIDGE
The Pitt Building, Trumpington Street, Cambridge, United Kingdom

CAMBRIDGE UNIVERSITY PRESS
The Edinburgh Building, Cambridge CB2 2RU, UK   http://www.cup.cam.ac.uk
40 West 20th Street, New York, NY 10011–4211, USA   http://www.cup.org
10 Stamford Road, Oakleigh, Melbourne 3166, Australia
Ruiz de Alarcón 13, 28014 Madrid, Spain

First published 1984
Second edition 1993
Ninth printing 1999

Printed in the United States of America

Typeset in Minion

Library of Congress Cataloging-in-Publication Data
Gilbert, Judy B. (Judy Bogen)
Clear Speech : pronunciation and listening comprehension in North
American English : student's book / Judy B. Gilbert. - 2nd ed.
p.cm.
ISBN 0-521-42118-7 (pbk.)
1. English language–Textbooks for foreign speakers. 2. English
language – United States – Pronunciation. 3. Listening. I. Title.
PE1128.G52 1993
428.3'4 – dc202   92-46240
                                                          CIP

A catalog record for this book is available from the British Library

ISBN 0–521–42118–7 (Student's Book)
ISBN 0–521–42116–0 (Teacher's Resource Book)
ISBN 0–521–42117–9 (Cassette Set)

Design, layouts, and text composition: Adventure House, Inc.
Illustrations
Daisy de Puthod: pages 28 (*top*), 31 (*bottom*), 66, 85
Luisa Kolla: pages 8, 9, 10, 12, 23, 35, 37, 38, 39, 118, 124, 125, 129
MM Design 2000, Inc.: pages 1, 25, 27, 28 (*middle*), 41, 45, 47, 48,
50, 51, 54, 60, 78, 83, 93, 97, 100, 102, 106, 107

Cassette production by The Sun Group. The recording of Louis Moreau
Gottschalk's "Pasquinade," played by Eugene List, courtesy of Omega
Record Group, Inc., New York, New York.

Contents

Acknowledgments

I would like to thank the more than seventy teachers who have given time and attention to field-testing the successive drafts of this new edition. Their efforts have been important in making this book easier to teach, and I gratefully acknowledge their institutions in the Teacher's Resource Book.

I am grateful to the following people who have offered valuable suggestions: William Acton, Roberta Adams, Janet Anderson-Hsieh, Heidi Broder-Berman, Cristin Carpenter, Rhoda Curtis, Rebecca Ford, Elisabeth Gareis, Janet Graham, Linda Grant, Brenda Prouser Imber, James Kirchner, Carole Mawson, David Mendelsohn, Alan Shaterian, Doris Shiffman, Earl Stevick, Judith Ward, and Rita Wong. My students in the ESL Certificate Program at University of California, Berkeley, were also a great help in this project as they tested successive versions of the book with their own students. Dr. J. C. Catford gave valuable advice on the descriptions of sounds. Remaining errors are my own.

I would also like to thank Alice Stiebel for her intelligent and practical testing of all drafts of the original book as well as this new edition. And I am grateful for the wise editing of Ellen Shaw, Sandra Graham, Suzette André, and my Anonymous Reviewer, and for the thoughtful assistance of Mary Vaughn.

Text credits

On page 26, "I think that I shall never see ...," in *The Burgess Nonsense Book,* by Gelett Burgess, 1901, reprinted by J. B. Lippincott Co.

On page 76, "These lines can show you ...," in *Rhyme's Reason* by John Hollander, 1981, Yale University Press.

On page 85, "Song of the Open Road," in *Happy Days,* by Ogden Nash, 1933, Simon and Schuster. Reprinted by permission of Curtis Brown, Ltd. Copyright 1931 by Ogden Nash. Also in *Collected Poems,* by Ogden Nash, Andre Deutsch Ltd.; *Verses From 1929 On,* by Ogden Nash. Copyright by Ogden Nash. By permission of Little, Brown and Co.

On page 97, "The Hippopotamus," in *I'm a Stranger Here Myself,* by Ogden Nash, 1938, Little, Brown and Co. Reprinted by permission of Curtis Brown, Ltd. Copyright 1935 by Ogden Nash. Also in *Collected Poems,* by Ogden Nash, Andre Deutsch Ltd.; *Verses From 1929 On,* by Ogden Nash. Copyright 1935 by The Curtis Publishing Co. First appeared in *The Saturday Evening Post.* By permission of Little, Brown and Co.

To the student

Do not worry about mastering the sounds of English in the beginning of this course. The sounds will improve as you practice the rhythm of English.

Symbols used in the text

Slashes identify reduced vowels.

> *Example* banana

An "*X*" signals silence of the letter "h" or of vowels.

> *Examples* Is ✗e busy? (sounds like "Izzybizzy?")
> clos✗d

Rising and falling lines indicate the pitch patterns of sentences.

> *Examples* Is she there?   Which car?

Bars and dots identify long and short syllables.

> *Example* record (noun)   record (verb)
> — •   • —

Bold type indicates stress.

> *Examples* I **want** a ba**na**na.
> A **stu**dent was **sent** to Ta**co**ma.

Cassettes

⊡ marks sections that are recorded on the cassettes.

To the teacher

Clear Speech, Second Edition, concentrates on rhythm, stress, and intonation because improvement in these aspects of pronunciation can do the most good in improving both listening comprehension and clarity of speech. Sounds are taught as part of rhythm and stress.

One of the key concepts that is emphasized in this new edition is *contractions and reductions*. Students are often reluctant to use contracted and reduced forms because they fear "sloppy speech" or because they feel they will leave out necessary information. This reluctance can form a considerable barrier to listening comprehension because contractions and reductions are a basic part of the information system of spoken English.

Difficult sounds are approached from a variety of perspectives. The sounds in Units 2 to 7 are not arranged in traditional sound pairs. They are presented in a form to help students learn to recognize some of the causes of their own difficulties, and to increase listening speed through improved recognition of sounds at the end of words. The final sound is often hard to hear and yet may convey important grammatical information.

Students believe that they will improve their pronunciation if they work hard on individual sounds. However, improving *rhythm* will do more for clarifying sounds than any amount of practice on the sounds themselves. That is why rhythm is introduced early into the units on sounds. It is recommended that you do not allow the class to be trapped in an effort to perfect individual sounds before moving on. The later units are much more important for increasing the clarity of your students' speech and listening comprehension.

Organization of units

The following are the kinds of activities you will find in *Clear Speech*:

Clear Listening and Clear Speaking Tests   One or both of these tests can provide information about skill areas that need improvement. The teacher's version of the Clear Listening Test, with directions, as well as analysis information and a student Pronunciation Profile form, is in the Teacher's Resource Book.

Pair practice   Pair practice activities function as a challenge to communication and give students – even in very large classes – the opportunity to practice speaking and hearing English. The correct answer depends on distinguishing between alternatives. Pair practice provides the immediate feedback so important to motivation. Moreover, it places more responsibility for learning where it belongs – with the student.

The teacher can circulate among pairs, giving help on a more personal basis. To provide variety, the pair practice can be used as a listening exercise or as a quiz, with you playing the part of Student 1, or one student can be Student 1 and the whole class can be Student 2.

Dictation   Taking dictation alerts students to areas of listening perception that still need improvement. You can read from the Teacher's Resource Book or use the cassettes. Interest can be enhanced by using dictation material from the students' own fields of study or work, or from current topical subjects.

Rhythm practice   Brief pieces of light poetry have been included to encourage a sense of flow of English rhythm. You may find other poetry (e.g., the lyrics of songs) more suited to your particular students. The class can listen to the teacher or the cassettes, then recite the poem as a group or as separate groups saying alternate lines. Rhythm practice is most effective when physical activity is included, such as marking time by tapping the table or moving the body in some way.

Review   Each unit ends with a review of a teaching point from an earlier unit, sometimes presented in a new aspect. Topics are reintroduced in order to refresh and solidify the earlier lessons.

Mouth illustrations

New mouth illustrations show the teeth and views from the side and above in order to help students become oriented to the visual information. The teacher should give students time to silently trace internally what they see in the drawings.

Exercise selection

This book was designed to be used in a wide range of teaching situations; therefore, you should feel free to choose those exercises that are most appropriate for your students. You may also wish to shorten some exercises if further practice is unnecessary.

Teacher's Resource Book

This companion book can enhance the teaching of the text because it provides practical explanations of the rationale for each lesson, useful classroom procedures, ready-made quizzes, answers for the exercises, and lectures for listening practice.

Clear Listening Test 📼

How you hear English is closely connected with how you speak English.

Part 1

Sounds

[10 points]

The following pairs of sentences are exactly the same except for one word. You will hear either sentence (a) or (b). Circle the letter of the sentence you hear.

Example a. Do you want everything?
     (b.) **Do you wash everything?**

1. a. They save old bottles.
   b. They saved old bottles.

2. a. She loves each child.
   b. She loved each child.

3. a. Was a bath all he wanted?
   b. Was a bat all he wanted?

4. a. He always spills everything.
   b. He always spilled everything.

5. a. Did she bring her card every day?
   b. Did she bring her car every day?

6. a. Which cuff do you like?
   b. Which cup do you like?

7. a. They've already gone.
   b. They'd already gone.

8. a. We can often see the mountains.
   b. We can't often see the mountains.

9. a. Who'll ask you?
   b. Who'd ask you?

10. a. We watch all of it.
    b. We wash all of it.

Part 2

Syllable number

[10 points]

How many syllables do you hear? Write the number.

Examples a.   ease   _1_
         b.   easy   _2_
         c.   easily   _3_

1. closet	____	6. opened	____
2. sport	____	7. first	____
3. clothes	____	8. caused	____
4. simplify	____	9. committee	____
5. frightened	____	10. arrangement	____

Part 3

Word stress

[10 points]

Draw a line under the syllable with the most stress (the strongest syllable). Mark only one syllable for each word.

Examples   a. de<u>lay</u>
　　　　　　 b. <u>bro</u>ken
　　　　　　 c. edu<u>ca</u>tion

1. participating	6. Europe
2. photograph	7. information
3. photography	8. economy
4. Canadian	9. economic
5. geography	10. political

Part 4

Contractions, reductions

[20 points]

You will hear a sentence. It will be read twice. Write the missing words.

Example   You hear: Do you think she's in her room?

　　　　　　 You write: Do you think _____*she's*_____ in her room?
　　　　　　　　　　　 or
　　　　　　　　　　　 Do you think _____*she is*_____ in her room?

1. _____ you ask?

2. _____ work good?

3. _____ you go?

4. Please _____ the information.

5. _____ everything.

6. _____

7. _____

8. _____

9. _____

10. _____

Part 5

Focus: identification   **[10 points]**

You will hear a dialogue with ten sentences. In each sentence underline the word with the most emphasis (the strongest word).

Example A: That's a **great** idea!

A: Do you think food in this country is expensive?
B: Not really.
A: I think it's expensive.
B: That's because you eat in restaurants.
A: Where do you eat?
B: At home.
A: Can you cook?
B: Well, actually I can't cook. I just eat cheese.
A: That's awful!

Part 6

Focus: meaning   **[20 points]**

The following pairs of sentences are exactly the same, except a different word is stressed (stronger) in each sentence. You will hear sentence (a) or (b) twice. Circle the correct response.

Example a. They bought two bottles.   Not three?
       b. **They bought two bottles.**   **Not cans?**

Teacher: Give students time to read these sentences first.

1. a. We want to buy a lot of apples.   Not oranges?
   b. We want to buy a lot of apples.   How many?

2. a. I think that animal is a wolf.   No, it's a fox.
   b. I think that animal is a wolf.   Aren't you sure?

3. a. Frank wanted to go early.   When?
   b. Frank wanted to go early.   Who?

4. a. Sally <u>writes</u> the reports.   No, she reviews them.
    b. Sally <u>writes</u> the reports.   No, Bob does.

5. a. Does <u>she</u> speak French?   No, but he does.
    b. Does she <u>speak</u> French?   No, but she can read it.

Part 7

Thought groups   [20 points]

You will hear sentence (a) or (b) twice. Answer the question that follows the sentence you hear.

Example a. John said, "My father is here."
          b. **"John," said my father, "is here."**
          Question Who was speaking?   _my father_

1. a. He sold his houseboat and car.
    b. He sold his house, boat, and car.
    Question How many things did he sell?   _____

2. a. She likes pineapples.
    b. She likes pie and apples.
    Question How many things does she like?   _____

3. a. Would you like some soup or salad?
    b. Would you like some Super Salad?
    Question How many things were you offered?   _____

4. a. The president said, "That reporter is lying."
    b. "The president," said that reporter, "is lying."
    Question Who was speaking?   _____

5. a. Wooden matches are used to start fires.
    b. Wood and matches are used to start fires.
    Question How many kinds of things are used
             to start fires?   _____

Clear Speaking Test

Record this dialogue. Speak in a conversational style, as naturally as possible.

At the Travel Agent's Office 📼

A: [1] Can I help you?

B: [2] Yes, I want to fly to Chicago on Wednesday the seventh and return on Friday the ninth.

A: [3] Of October?

B: [4] No, November. How much is the fare?

A: [5] Fares are cheaper if you stay over Saturday night.

B: [6] Thanks, but unfortunately I've already arranged some business here that Friday. So I'll just have to pay the extra cost.

A: [7] What time of day would you prefer? Morning or afternoon?

B: [8] Morning, because I have to be there by early evening. Is there a meal?

A: [9] Yes, they'll be serving breakfast; and you'll also see a movie.

B: [10] Which movie?

A: [11] In both directions they'll show a short feature on planned communities. [12] Going east, the major film is *City Slickers*. [13] I think it's a cowboy comedy. [14] The movie going west is *Big Joe*. [15] That's an adventure story about a boy who raises a wolf.

B: [16] Sounds good, but what's the fare?

A: [17] Eight hundred and fifty dollars round trip.

B: [18] That's more than I expected!

1 Rhythm: number of syllables

How many syllables are in this word? sandwich _____

How many syllables are in this sentence? Send a witch. _____

A
Counting syllables

The basic unit of English rhythm is the syllable. Languages have different rules about the ways syllables are spoken.

Listen to the following words. Tap the desk for each syllable.

1 syllable	2 syllables	3 syllables	4 syllables
ease	easy	easily	
will	willing	willingly	
care	careful	carefully	
one	seven	eleven	identify
two	eighteen	direction	analysis
name	sentence	syllable	It's important.
called	focus	emphasis	He wants a book.
can't	cannot		
	happy	happiness	
	Send which?	Send a witch.	

B
Pair practice

Student 1 says a word from list 1 or list 2. Student 2 says the matching word from the other list. Take turns being Student 1. Do not always choose list 1 first.

Example Student 1: sit
            Student 2: city

Note Some of these pairs of words have different vowels. However, the most important cause of confusion between these words is the number of syllables.

1	2	1	2
sit	city	dish	dishes
fish	fishy	state	estate
blow	below	flow	fellow
prayed	parade	clothes	cloth is
loud	aloud	steam	esteem
closed	closet	through	thorough
sport	support	squeeze	excuse
cracked	correct	sleep	asleep
first	forest	school	a school
cleaned	clean it	train	terrain
rose	roses	miss	misses
choose	chooses	watch	watches

C

Counting syllables in a sentence

Decide how many syllables are in each sentence. Compare your list with a partner. Then practice the sentences aloud.

1. Buy a washing machine. ___6___
2. Where is the electrical panel? ___9___
3. Do we need a garage mechanic? ___9___
4. Students in school must study. ___7___
5. Computer programming is a good profession. ___12___
6. Automobile parts are made in many countries. ___
7. They closed the department store in August. ___
8. We rented it before noon. ___

[handwritten notes in right margin:] Now read them as beats — w/ linking. How many beats per sentence?

D

Pair practice: sentences

Read the following sentences. Then take turns challenging a partner. Student 1 says question (a) or (b). Student 2 says the matching answer. Take turns being Student 1. Do not always choose question (a).

Note It is useful to practice spelling aloud quickly and clearly.

Examples   Student 1: How do you spell "support"?
Student 2: S U P P O R T

Student 1: What does "steam" mean?
Student 2: Vapor from boiling water.

1.   a. How do you spell "sport"?   S P O R T
     b. How do you spell "support"?   S U P P O R T

2.   a. What does "steam" mean?   Vapor from boiling water.
     b. What does "esteem" mean?   Respect.

3.   a. What does "closed" mean?   The opposite of "open."
     b. What does "closet" mean?   A place to put things.

4.   a. How do you spell "through"?   T H R O U G H
     b. How do you spell "thorough"?   T H O R O U G H

5.   a. Where is the first?   At the beginning.
     b. Where is the forest?   In the mountains.

6.   a. Did you bring the dish?   Yes, just one.
     b. Did you bring the dishes?   Yes, all of them.

7.   a. What does "traffic" mean?   Lots of cars.
     b. What does "terrific" mean?   Wow!

8.   a. What does "cracked" mean?   Something like "broken,"
     b. What does "correct" mean?   Right.

E

Grammar: the past tense 🔲

The endings of words are important in English grammar. Look at how "-ed" changes the verbs below.

Present tense ——————————▶ **Past tense**
    rent   rented

1 Listen to the following words. Hold up 1 finger if you hear 1 syllable, and 2 fingers if you hear 2 syllables.

planted	landed	worked	caused	planned
laughed	added	folded	treated	counted
started	watched	closed	opened	cooked

Sometimes "-ed" is pronounced as an extra syllable, and sometimes it is not. Can you figure out the rule for this? If not, work the following puzzle.

2 *Puzzle* What do all of the verbs in list A have in common? In list B? The verbs in C and D do not have an extra syllable in the past tense. How are they different from the verbs in A and B?

A	B	C	D
plant	land	work	wash
start	fold	live	walk
treat	add	save	cause
wait	fade	laugh	plan
heat	load	call	close
attract	record	arrange	contain

3 Write the past tense of these verbs. Count the number of syllables.

	Past tense	Syllables		Past tense	Syllables
paint	_____	___	open	_____	___
rent	_____	___	close	_____	___
need	_____	___	like	_____	___
want	_____	___	dislike	_____	___
decide	_____	___	clean	_____	___
select	_____	___	return	_____	___
visit	_____	___	work	_____	___
represent	_____	___	call	_____	___
intend	_____	___	practice	_____	___

Rule If the last sound of a regular verb is **T** or **D**, the past tense has an extra syllable.

F

Pair practice

Student 1 says sentence (a) or (b). Do not choose the same letter each time. Student 2 says "past" or "present."

Examples Student 1: We need more money.
Student 2: Present.

Student 1: We started early.
Student 2: Past.

1. a. We need more money.
    b. We needed more money.

2. a. We start early.
    b. We started early.

3. a. The doctors treat patients.
    b. The doctors treated patients.

4. a. We rent a house every summer.
    b. We rented a house every summer.

5. a. They start at 10 o'clock.
    b. They started at 10 o'clock.

6. a. The teachers want a pay raise.
    b. The teachers wanted a pay raise.

7. a. I intend to go shopping.
    b. I intended to go shopping.

8. a. People crowd into the trains.
    b. People crowded into the trains.

9. a. Children skate on the frozen lake.
    b. Children skated on the frozen lake.

10. a. They regularly visit the library.
    b. They regularly visited the library.

G

Dropped syllables

Listen to these words. Draw an X through the silent letters.* Then read the words aloud.

Examples   openeᗪ   chocᗶlate
             walkeᗪ

1 syllable	2 syllables	3 syllables	4 syllables
walked	chocolate	vegetable	laboratory
planned	several	interesting	elementary
closed	business		
talked	Wednesday		
	every		

*These are common pronunciations in North America, but some English speakers may say these words differently.

Now listen to how the British say
chocolate
several
interesting
laboratory
elementary

Can find themselves in the middle

5

H

Dictation

Listen to these sentences. Write the words you hear. Then count the number of syllables for each sentence. You will hear each sentence two times.

Number of syllables in the sentence

Example   Go tell the teacher.   5

1.   Vegetables are expensive at the present time.   12
2.   Does she go to Alaska often   8

not from tape
3.   John. said his father was home   7
4.   Is there a tomatoe in the refrigerator ?   13
5.   How much do you like photography ?   9

I

Check your progress

Write the number of syllables over the underlined words. If you have a tape recorder, record yourself saying these sentences.

This is the <u>first</u> <u>city</u> they <u>visited</u> when they <u>traveled</u> here on <u>business</u>, and they

were so <u>pleased</u> that they <u>added</u> two more stops.

J

Syllable number game

The class can be divided into teams, or each student can race against time. In five minutes, how many foods can you think of that have 1, 2, or 3 syllables? Put them in columns like this:

1 syllable	2 syllables	3 syllables
rice	carrot	banana
bread	butter	coconut
milk	hot dog	hamburger
_____	_____	_____
_____	_____	_____
_____	_____	_____

Another possible category: countries and capitals.

1 syllable	2 syllables	3 syllables
France	Sweden	Italy
Spain	China	Canada
Rome	Paris	Washington
_____	_____	_____
_____	_____	_____
_____	_____	_____

2 Stops and continuants

Look at the parts of the mouth in this picture.

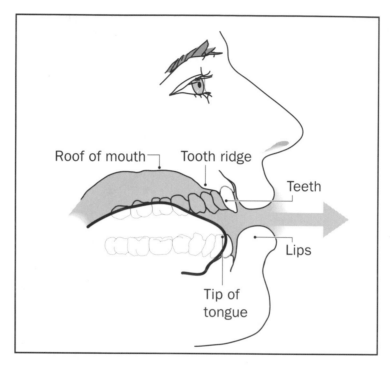

Different sounds are made by the way the air flows over the tongue. When the tongue touches different parts of the mouth, the air flow changes, which changes the sound.

In some sounds we let the air flow through without stopping – **continuant sounds**. Say this word and make the final sound continue:

BUSssssssssssssss

In other sounds, we stop the air flow inside the mouth – **stop sounds**. Say this word and feel the way the final sound must stop:

BUT

Practice feeling the difference between these two sounds.

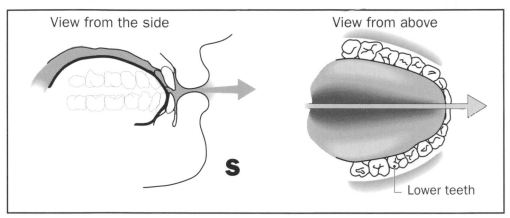

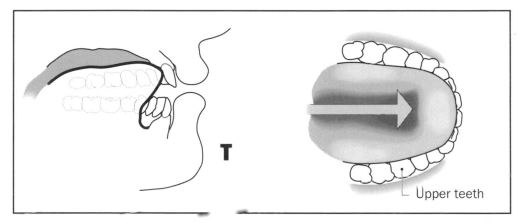

Silently feel the difference between the final sound of "bus" and "but." In one you can feel the air flow out. In the other, the air is stopped.

Now *silently* practice alternating these sounds: "Sss, T, Sss, T, Sss, T, Sss, T, bus, but, bus, but." Then practice saying these words out loud.

A

The sounds in words 🔲

Practice saying these word pairs. Feel the difference between the final sounds.

Continuant	Stop	Continuant	Stop
bus	but	nice	night
rice	right	race	rate
mice	might	boss	bought

B

TH *and* T

Below are pictures of **TH** and **T**. In **TH**, the tongue is flat and relaxed. *Silently* try out the difference between **TH** and **T**.

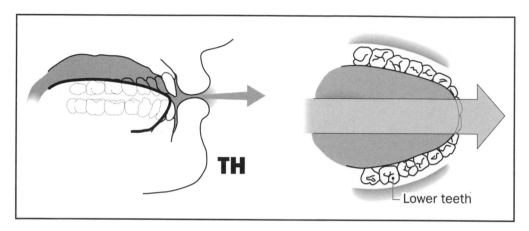

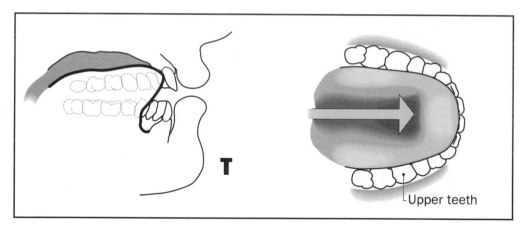

In **TH**, the flat tip of the tongue briefly touches the upper front teeth. The air continues to flow out of the mouth. This makes a continuant sound: **TH**. Feel air moving quietly over the tongue and teeth.

Now raise your tongue and press against the tooth ridge all around so that the air cannot flow out. This makes a stop sound: **T**.

Silently practice changing from one sound to another: "TH, T, TH, T, TH, T, bath, bat, bath, bat." Then practice the sounds out loud.

C

Pair practice: words with TH and T

Student 1 says a word from list 1 or list 2. Student 2 indicates the word that was heard by saying "one" or "two."

Note Do not always choose list 1 first because then it is too easy for your partner.

Example Student 1: bat
Student 2: two

1 Continuant	2 Stop
bath	bat
both	boat
booth	boot
faith	fate
Ruth	root

D

Pair practice: sentences with TH and T

Student 1 says sentence (a) or (b). Student 2 says the matching answer.

1. a. What does "path" mean?   A place to walk
   b. What does "pat" mean?   Tap.

2. a. What is a bath for?   To get clean.
   b. What is a bat for?   To play ball.

3. a. How do you spell "both"?   B O T H
   b. How do you spell "boat"?   B O A T

4. a. What does "faith" mean?   Belief.
   b. What does "fate" mean?   Destiny.

5. a. How do you spell "mat"?   M A T
   b. How do you spell "math"?   M A T H

6. a. What does "wrath" mean?   Anger.
   b. What does "rat" mean?   Like a mouse.

7. a. Where is the booth?   At the fair.
   b. Where is the boot?   On my foot.

8. a. How do you spell "Ruth"?   R U T H
   b. How do you spell "root"?   R O O T

E

R *and* D

The continuant sound in the following picture is a North American **R** (U.S. and Canada). The tip of the tongue *must not stop the air*. The air flows out over the tip of the tongue.

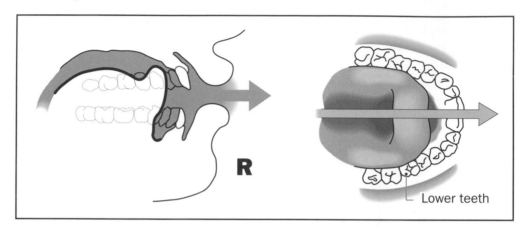

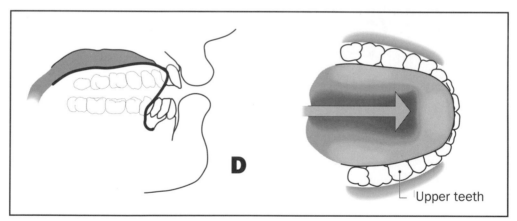

Silently do this:

- Raise your tongue so that you feel the sides of the tongue touch the tooth ridge toward the back of the mouth.

- Do not let the tip of your tongue touch any other part of your mouth.

This makes a continuant sound: **R**.

Now *silently* raise your whole tongue so that you are pressing the tooth ridge all around and the air cannot flow out. This makes a stop sound: **D**.

Alternate making these sounds silently: "Rrr, D, Rrr, D, Rrr, D." Now practice making the sounds out loud: "bar, bad, bar, bad."

F
Pair practice: words with R and D

Student 1 says a word from list 1 or list 2. Student 2 says the other word.

At the beginning of words:

1	2
red	dead
ran	Dan
rot	dot
row	dough
room	doom
rust	dust

At the end of words:

1	2
hire	hide
fear	feed
bear	bed
dare	dead
fear	feared
car	card
care	cared
share	shared
prepare	prepared
retire	retired

G
Pair practice: sentences with R and D

Student 1 says question (a) or (b). Student 2 says the matching answer.

Beginning sound:

1. a. What color is rust? Usually orange.
   b. What color is dust? Usually gray.

2. a. How do you spell "row"? R O W
   b. How do you spell "dough"? D O U G H

3. a. What's a dam? A wall for water.
   b. What's a ram? A male sheep.

Ending sound:

4. a. What does "fear" mean? To be scared.
   b. What does "feed" mean? To give food.

5. a. Where's the bear? In the zoo.
   b. Where's the bed? In the bedroom.

6. a. Where's the car? On the road.
   b. Where's the card? On the table.

7. a. What does "we're" mean?   We are.
    b. What does "weed" mean?   A plant nobody wants.

8. a. How do you spell "tire"?   T I R E
    b. How do you spell "tied"?   T I E D

H

Linking practice: R

English speakers connect many words by linking them together. For example, say "hear us." In slow speech it sounds like this: "hearrrus." The **R** sound continues until it links the two words together.

1 Practice linking these words together.

hear us	pair of	tear it
fire in	share of	we're all

2 Practice linking these sentences together.

1. Do you hear us?
2. There is a fire in the oven.
3. We need a pair of shoes.
4. Do you want to share a taxi?
5. Tear it out of the newspaper.
6. We're all ready to go.

I

Linking practice: D

Practice linking the stop sound **D** to the vowel that follows it. You cannot continue a stop sound, so linking the two words makes the stop sound seem like the beginning of the next word. Practice with linking words can help you understand spoken English faster.

Examples "had it" sounds like "hadit"
            "thank you" sounds like "thankyou"
            "paid Ann" sounds like "paidAnn"

1 Practice linking these words together.

had it	told us	had always
said everything	did only	paid Ann

2 Practice linking these sentences together.

1. I had it this morning.
2. She said everything.
3. You told us last week.
4. I did only the first part.
5. She had always wanted to sing.
6. They paid Ann yesterday.

J
Rhythm practice: **R** *and* **D**

Say this limerick, paying attention to the final sounds in "Niger," "tiger," "ride," and "inside."

Note The "g" in "Niger" is pronounced like the "j" in "jet." In "tiger," it is pronounced like the "g" in "get."

> There was a young lady from Niger
> Who went for a ride on a tiger;
>   They returned from the ride
>   With the lady inside,
> And a smile on the face of the tiger.
>
>   (Anonymous)

K
Check your progress: dictation

1. _____
2. _____
3. _____
4. _____
5. _____

Review
Number of syllables

Count the syllables in these sentences. Then practice the dialogue with a partner. Stress the underlined words to make the dialogue sound natural.

Number of syllables

Tired Tourists	*3*
X: Maybe we planned to do too much.	___
Y: Yes, but I wanted to see <u>more</u>.	___
X: <u>You</u> were the one who decided to stop.	___
Y: Well, I needed to rest.	___
X: And <u>I</u> wanted to continue!	___

3 More stops and continuants: grammar

A
Pair practice with R and D: past or present?

Pay attention to the verbs in the following sentences. If these verbs end in a stop sound, the sentence is in the past.

Student 1 says sentence (a) or (b). Student 2 says "past" or "present."

Example Student 1: We shared all the food.
Student 2: Past.

1. a. We share all the food.
   b. We shared all the food. P
2. a. The dogs scare every cat.
   b. The dogs scared every cat.
3. a. Some speakers bore us.
   b. Some speakers bored us.
4. a. They hire new employees on Friday.
   b. They hired new employees on Friday.
5. a. They fear every animal.
   b. They feared every animal.
6. a. The children share each cookie.
   b. The children shared each cookie.
7. a. We admire all your work.
   b. We admired all your work.
8. a. They pour milk into the glass.
   b. They poured milk into the glass.
9. a. Do you think they care about politics?
   b. Do you think they cared about politics?

B
Pair practice with D and continuants: past or present?

Pay attention to the final sound of the verb. Is it a stop or a continuant? Student 1 says sentence (a) or (b). Student 2 says "past" or "present."

a or b?

1.
2.
3.
4.
5

a   or   b?

Example   Student 1: They close everything.
           Student 2: Present.

1.

1. (a.) They close everything.
    b. They closed everything.

2.

2. a. They close all shops on Wednesday.
    (b.) They closed all shops on Wednesday.

3.

3. a. The baby cries all the time.
    (b.) The baby cried all the time.

4.

4. (a.) He pays all the bills.
    b. He paid all the bills.

5.

5. (a.) I rush every morning.
    b. I rushed every morning.

6. a. We join our group on Saturday.
    b. We joined our group on Saturday.

7. a. They fix every car.
    b. They fixed every car.

8. a. We practice every Friday.
    b. We practiced every Friday.

9. a. They miss each one.
    b. They missed each one.

10. a. We save all your letters.
    b. We saved all your letters.

11. a. We wash our car.
    b. We washed our car.

C

Pair practice with S and stops: singular or plural?

Pay attention to the final sound of the noun.

Student 1 says sentence (a) or (b). Student 2 says "singular" or "plural."

Example   Student 1: Read your books.
           Student 2: Plural.

a   or   b?

1.

1. a. Read your book.
    (b.) Read your books.

2.

2. a. Bring your map tomorrow.
    (b.) Bring your maps tomorrow.

3. a. Copy your report each day.
   b. Copy your reports each day.

4. a. I put the ticket in my pocket.
   b. I put the tickets in my pocket.

5. a. Where did you put the cake?
   b. Where did you put the cakes?

6. a. Did you enjoy your trip?
   b. Did you enjoy your trips?

7. a. Poison the rat!
   b. Poison the rats!

8. a. Clean the rug now.
   b. Clean the rugs now.

9. a. Fill the tub with hot water.
   b. Fill the tubs with hot water.

10. a. Did somebody move the bed?
    b. Did somebody move the beds?

D

Linking practice: continuants 📼

Speak slowly to help yourself concentrate on the continuant sound that links the two words:

"bus all"   =   "busssall"
"can always"   =   "cannnalways"

S	R	TH	N
face any	fair answer	math is	can allow
space age	share any	both of	can even
this ice	scare it	faith in	can always

Practice these sentences.

1. This is a space age project.
2. That wasn't a fair answer.
3. Both of you can accept money.
4. We can always share a taxi.
5. They can allow that.
6. There's something in this ice!

E

Linking practice: stops 🔲

Link the final stop to the next word:

"stop it"   = "stopit"
"can't always" = "can'talways"

B	P	D	T	G	K
rob all	top of	had other	fit any	bag of	back of
tub of	stop it	made it	lot of	tag every	lock all
			can't allow		
			can't ever		
			can't accept		

Practice these sentences.

1. They had other plans.
2. Lock all the doors.
3. I want you to stop it!

4. We can't allow robbers to rob us.
5. I can't accept the money.
6. You can't always win.

F

V *and* B

Look at the lips and teeth in these pictures.

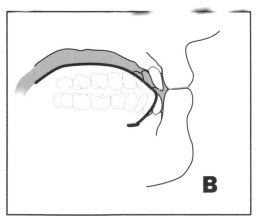
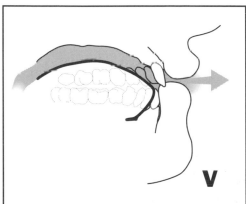

Practice these sounds *silently*. If you close your lips for the **B** sound, no air can come out.

To make the **V** sound, press the inner part of the lower lip against the front of the upper teeth. If you have trouble keeping your lips apart for the **V** sound, place a pencil or your finger across the lower lip to remind you to keep the lips apart.

When you understand how the sounds are made, practice them out loud.

G

Pair practice: words with V *and* B

Student 1 says a word from list 1 or list 2. Student 2 says the other word.

1	2		1	2
vet	bet		rove	robe
very	berry		curve	curb
vat	bat			
vote	boat			

H

Pair practice: sentences with V *and* B

Student 1 says sentence (a) or (b). Student 2 answers.

1. a. He wants to buy my boat. Will you sell it?
   b. He wants to buy my vote. That's against the law!

2. a. What's a bat? A flying mouse.
   b. What's a vat? A container for liquid.

3. a. What does "vend" mean? To sell.
   b. What does "bend" mean? To curve.

4. a. Where's the vase? On the table.
   b. Where's the base? At the bottom.

5. a. What does "marvel" mean? An amazing thing.
   b. What does "marble" mean? A kind of stone.

6. a. What's a curve? A bend.
   b. What's a curb? An edge to the road.

I

Linking practice: V *and* B

1 Practice saying these words.

have‿an   save‿us   believe‿it   rob‿us   cab‿is

2 Draw linking lines to words that begin with vowels. Then say the sentences.

1. I don't have any.
2. Who can save us?

3. Don't you believe it?
4. Will he shave off his beard?
5. His white dove is flying with five others.
6. We can't allow robbers to rob us!
7. The cab is coming soon.
8. Here is a bag of candy.
9. We had all that we wanted.
10. Would anybody like tea?

J

Pair practice: dialogue

Note Be careful with **V** and **B**.

  The Great Athlete

X: Do you like to play volleyball?
Y: Not very much.
X: But it's fun!
Y: I can't serve the ball.
X: Maybe you just need practice.
Y: But I can't get the ball over the net.
X: Never?
Y: Hardly ever. Besides that, I bump into the other players.
X: Mmmmm. Then maybe you should play bridge.

K

Pair practice: **V** *and* **D**

Student 1 says a word from list 1 or list 2. Student 2 says the other word.

1	2
have	had
live	lid
leave	lead
save	saved
live	lived
love	loved
believe	believed

L

Pair practice: past or present?

Rule Vowels at the beginning of words are like magnets for the final sound of the word that comes before.

Note All of the verbs in the sentences below are followed by a vowel. If you link the verb to the following word, you will sound more like an English speaker.

Student 1 says sentence (a) or (b). Student 2 says "past" or "present." Pay attention to the ending sounds of the verbs.

1. a. They save old bottles.
    b. They saved old bottles.

2. a. They believe everything.
    b. They believed everything.

3. a. We live in an apartment.
    b. We lived in an apartment.

4. a. We have a big car.
    b. We had a big car.

5. a. They love animals.
    b. They loved animals.

6. a. Many men shave every day.
    b. Many men shaved every day.

7. a. Highway workers pave our roads.
    b. Highway workers paved our roads.

8. a. Some dogs retrieve all balls.
    b. Some dogs retrieved all balls.

9. a. Rude people shove into lines.
    b. Rude people shoved into lines.

10. a. We approve all her work.
    b. We approved all her work.

M
D *and* L

Following are pictures of **D** and **L**. The sound **L** is a continuant. Notice how the air flows out around the tip of the tongue.

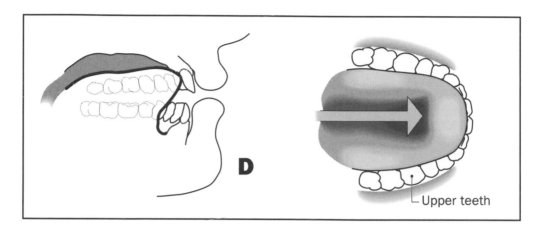

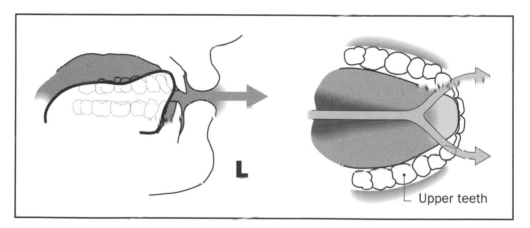

Silently make a **D** by pressing the tongue against the tooth ridge all around. Hold it until you can feel that the air flow is stopped.

Now make an **L** this way: Keep the tip of the tongue pressed against the tooth ridge in front, but lower the rest of the tongue. This allows the air to flow over the tongue and out on both sides of the raised tip. Breathe in and feel the cold air going back over the sides of the tongue.

Practice alternating these two positions until you know very well how they feel. Then practice making the sounds out loud: "bad, ball, bad, ball, bad, ball."

N

Pair practice with D and L

Student 1 says a word from list 1 or list 2. Student 2 says the other word.

1	2		1	2
wide	while		road	roll
raid	rail		made	mail
read	real		feed	feel

O

Check your progress: dictation

1. We share all our work.
2. She joined every club that interested her.
3. I rushed around to get ready on time.
4. Bring a book to read because the trains are always late.
5. They saved all five of our old letters.
6. We believe everything you tell us.

Summary

Stops and continuants

English stops: P T K
                 B D G

English continuants: All other sounds ⟶

Review

Linking

1 Practice linking these words:

what are	bag of	share any	kind of
beef on a	cake and	it's all	attitude is

2 Draw linking marks in the dialogue, then practice with a partner.

Two Friends in the Cafeteria

X: What are you having for lunch?
Y: Barbecue beef on a roll, a bag of chips, cake, and coffee.
X: Would you be willing to share any of your sandwich?
Y: No, it's all for me.
X: What kind of attitude is that?
Y: A selfish attitude!

4 Rhythm: stops and syllable length

Say these words. In speech, the first word is shorter than the second, even though the first word has more letters.

meant   men
·   —

Rule If the final sound is a stop, the vowel before it will be shorter.

light

If the final sound is a continuant, the vowel before will be longer.

line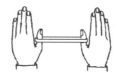

Vowels are continuant sounds:

meat   me
·   —

bite   buy
·   —

A
Making the sounds in words

Listen and then practice saying these words. Think about the length. Stretch a wide rubber band to help you concentrate on lengthening the words in list 2.

1	2
meat	me

1	2	1	2	1	2	1	2
·	—	·	—	·	—	·	—
bite	buy	seat	see	fight	fine	put	pull
white	why	plate	play	light	line	mate	main
light	lie	date	day	like	lics	cake	came
heat	he	note	no	feet	feel	rope	roll
keep	key	soap	so	seat	seal	boat	bone

25

B

Pair practice: stop or continuant?

Student 1 says question (a) or (b). Student 2 says the matching answer. Pay attention to the final sound. If it is a continuant, lengthen the vowel. (Remember: Vowels are continuants.)

Orally in class

1. a. How do you spell "suit"? S U I T
   b. How do you spell "Sue"? S U E

2. a. Where's the plate? On the table.
   b. Where's the play? At the theater.

3. a. What's the opposite of "light"? Dark.
   b. What's the opposite of "lie"? Truth.

4. a. What does "weak" mean? Not strong.
   b. What does "we" mean? Us.

5. a. What's a bat? A flying animal.
   b. What's a bath? A way to get clean.

6. a. What does "brought" mean? The past of "bring."
   b. What does "broth" mean? Clear soup.

7. a. How do you spell "white"? W H I T E
   b. How do you spell "why"? W H Y

8. a. What's a seat for? To sit on.
   b. What's a sea for? To swim in.

C

Rhythm practice 🔲

1 Practice lengthening one-syllable words ending in continuant sounds: "saw, cow, see, one, how, be."

2 One good way to practice the following poem is by whispering instead of speaking. Whispering will help you concentrate on the lengthening.

The Purple Cow

I never saw a purple cow,
I never hope to see one.
But, I can tell you anyhow,
I'd rather see than be one.

(Gelett Burgess)

Pair practice: words with D and L

Student 1 says a word from list 1 or list 2. Student 2 says the other word.

 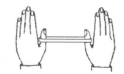

1	2
food	fool
paid	pale
rude	rule
seed	seal
they'd	they'll

E

Pair practice: sentences

Student 1 says question (a) or (b). Student 2 says the matching answer.

1. a. How do you spell "need."   N E E D
   b. How do you spell "kneel."   K N E E L

2. a. What does "they'll" mean?   They will.
   b. What does "they'd" mean?   They would.

3. a. What does "rule" mean?   To govern.
   b. What does "rude" mean?   Not polite.

4. a. What does "fell" mean?   The past of "fall."
   b. What does "fed" mean?   The past of "feed."

5. a. What's the opposite of "well"?   Sick.
   b. What's the opposite of "wed"?   Unmarried.

6. a. How do you spell "feel"?   F E E L
   b. How do you spell "field"?   F I E L D

7. a. Why did she feed it?   It was hungry.
   b. Why did she feel it?   To see if it was hot.

8. a. What does "fail" mean?   Not to succeed.
   b. What does "failed" mean?   The past of "fail."

F

Rhythm: contractions (D and L)

Contractions are common in spoken English. For example:

I would eat	=	I'd eat
I will eat	=	I'll eat
would	=	"d"
will	=	"l"

Note You do not need to use contractions in your own speech, but you do need to understand contractions when you hear them. Most English speakers use contractions all the time.

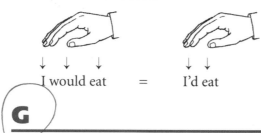

↓ ↓ ↓   ↓ ↓
I would eat   =   I'd eat

G

Listening practice with D and L: full or contracted? 🔲

Full word	Contraction
did, had, would (I would)	'd (I'd)
will (I will)	'll (I'll)

You will hear either sentence (a) or (b). Underline the full word from the sentence you hear.

Example You hear: They'd ask a good question.   will   <u>would</u>

Or you hear: They'll ask a good question.   <u>will</u>   would

Now listen.

1. a. They'll ask a good question.   will   would
   b. They'd ask a good question.

2. a. He'll answer soon.
    b. He'd answer soon.

(will) would

3. a. We'll prefer to pay cash.
    b. We'd prefer to pay cash.

will (would)

4. a. Do you think they'll like it?
    b. Do you think they'd like it?

will (would)

5. a. I said I'll do the work.
    b. I said I'd do the work.

(will) would

6. a. Who'll they ask?
    b. Who'd they ask?

will (did)

7. a. Where'll Ann find one?
    b. Where'd Ann find one?

will (did)

8. a. Perhaps he'll agree.
    b. Perhaps he'd agree.

(will) would

9. a. Do you suppose she'll come?
    b. Do you suppose she'd come?

will (would)

10. a. Where'll you put it?
    b. Where'd you put it?

(will) did

H

Check yourself

Record this dialogue. Pay attention to the length of your syllables.

These words are extra long:

two hours
have
leave
dare
do
bye

Too late for the lunch appointment

X: I've been waiting for two hours!
Y: You have? I'm sorry.
X: So I've decided to leave.
Y: You wouldn't dare!
X: That's just what I'm going to do. Bye!

Review

Dictation: stops and continuants 🔲

1. _____

2. _____

3. _____

4. _____

5. _____

 **Voicing**

The sound a snake makes: *hiss*

The sound a bee makes: *buzz*

Press your fingers against your ears and say this word, continuing the final **S** until you hear it clearly.

hiss   (unvoiced)

Now press your fingers against your ears and say this word, continuing the final **Z** until you hear the difference from the **S**.

buzz   (voiced)

The buzzing of the **Z** sound is called **voicing**. When you whisper, you are not voicing any of the sounds.

Practice changing from the voiced to the unvoiced sounds: "Sss, Zzz, Sss, Zzz, bus, buzz, bus, buzz, bus, buzz."

A
S and Z

1 Practice the following pairs of words.

Beginning sound		Final sound		Middle sound	
Unvoiced	Voiced	Unvoiced	Voiced	Unvoiced	Voiced
Sue	zoo	bus	buzz	lacy	lazy
sip	zip	Miss	Ms.	racing	raising
sink	zinc	rice	rise	bussing	buzzing

2 Listen to three words. One word has a different sound. Mark a check under the number for the word that is different.

Examples

			1	2	3
Sue	zoo	zoo	✓		
buzz	bus	buzz		✓	

	1	2	3
1.			✓
2.		✓	
3.			✓
4.		✓	
5.	✓		
6.			✓

B

Linking practice: S and Z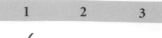

Listen to how the sound is linked to the vowel that follows.

Note The letter "s" is sometimes pronounced as a voiced sound, for example, "is."

Unvoiced (UV)	**Voiced (V)**
1. How nice͜ of you to come!	6. His͜ aunt called.
2. Would you like a piece͜ of pie?	7. My eyes͜ are tired.
3. Snakes hiss͜ out of fear.	8. Where is͜ Ann?
4. We eat rice͜ every day.	9. Was͜ all of it eaten?
5. Billy left a mess͜ in the sink.	10. Has͜ everybody left?

C

Mixed practice: voiced and unvoiced

Practice saying these sentences. Be careful with the voiced and unvoiced sounds.

1. The mouse͜ is͜ eating the rice͜ in the cupboard.
   (UV V   UV)

2. Was͜ all of his͜ office͜ a mess?
   (V   V   UV   UV)

we do.

D
Dialogue

1 Practice the contrast between voiced and unvoiced sounds.

Voiced	Unvoiced
buzzing noise	sound / hissing sound
bees	snake / sort of snake / sand snake
desert / middle of the desert	guess that's
amazing / amazing, isn't it?	

Mixed Voiced and Unvoiced

UV   V   V   UV UV   V   UV   V
sounds like bees   so surprising   that's amazing

2 Say the dialogue with a partner. Listen carefully to the voiced and unvoiced sounds.

In the Desert

A: What's that buzzing noise?
B: It sounds like bees.
A: But we're in the middle of the desert!
B: Yeah. That's amazing!
A: And what's that hissing sound?
B: Sounds like a snake.
A: A snake! What sort of snake?
B: A sand snake. They're very common here.
A: Well, I guess that's not so surprising.

E
Pair practice: words with V *and* F

Student 1 says a word from list 1 or list 2. Student 2 says "one" or "two."

Beginning sounds		Ending sounds		Middle sounds	
1 (voiced)	2 (unvoiced)	1 (voiced)	2 (unvoiced)	1 (voiced)	2 (unvoiced)
van	fan	leave	leaf	leaving	leafing
vine	fine	save	safe	service	surface
veil	fail	have	half	never	waffle
vine	fine	prove	proof	river	safer
"v"	fee	believe	belief	saving	rougher

33

F

Pair practice: sentences

Student 1 says question (a) or (b). Student 2 says the matching answer.

1. a. What does "fine" mean?   Something like "good."
   b. What does "vine" mean?   A kind of plant.

2. a. What does "veil" mean?   A covering for the face.
   b. What does "fail" mean?   The opposite of "succeed."

3. a. How do you spell "have"?   H A V E
   b. How do you spell "half"?   H A L F

4. a. What's a "v"?   A letter of the alphabet.
   b. What's a fee?   Cost for a service.

5. a. How do you spell "believe"?   B E L I E V E
   b. How do you spell "belief"?   B E L I E F

6. a. What does "fear" mean?   To be afraid.
   b. What does "veer" mean?   To change direction fast.

7. a. Do you have a view?   Yes, I can see the lake.
   b. Do you have a few?   No, I don't have any.

8. a. What's a "volley"?   A shot in tennis.
   b. What's a "folly"?   A foolish act.

G

Linking practice: **V, F, and TH** 🔲

Listen to how these sounds link to the vowel that follows.

Voiced
[V] love all   save us   give away   prove it   they've asked

Unvoiced
[F] laugh a lot   safe airplane   half empty   rough action
[TH] both are   fourth of   path along the river   teeth of animals

H
P *and* F

These sounds are made the same way as for **B** and **V**, but they are not voiced.

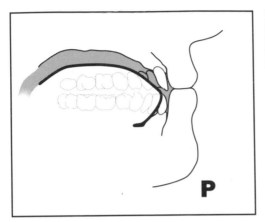 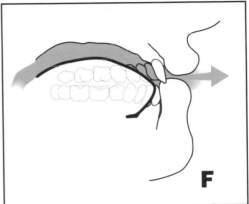

Practice saying the following words.

Beginning sound		Ending sound	
pair	fair	wipe	wife
pool	fool	lap	laugh
past	fast	clip	cliff
pail	fail	leap	leaf

For further practice on **P** and **F**, see Appendix B.

I
Pair practice: contractions to V, D, *and* L

Note Say the contractions aloud. This will help you hear them easily.

Student 1 says sentence (a) or (b). Student 2 says the full word.

Example Student 1: They'd gone.
　　　　　Student 2: had

1. a. They've gone.　　　have　　had
　　b. They'd gone.

2. a. We'd eaten.　　　　had　　have
　　b. We've eaten.

1.
2.
have (had)
had (have)

3. a. Where'd you put it?   did   (will)   have
    b. Where'll you put it?
    c. Where've you put it?

4. a. We'll come.   will   had   (have)
    b. We'd come.
    c. We've come.

5. a. How've you come here?   have   (did)   will
    b. How'd you come here?
    c. How'll you come here?

6. a. We'll shut the door.   (will)   had   have
    b. We'd shut the door.
    c. We've shut the door.

7. a. He's quit his job.   (has)   will   had
    b. He'll quit his job.
    c. He'd quit his job.

8. a. She's hurt her hand.   (has)   will   had
    b. She'll hurt her hand.
    c. She'd hurt her hand.

9. a. They've put it away.   (have)   will   had
    b. They'll put it away.
    c. They'd put it away.

10. a. Why'll you come?   will   (did)   have
    b. Why'd you come?
    c. Why've you come?

Review

Rhythm practice: stops and continuants

Practice making the contrast between **TH** and **T** and the combination sound **J**.

Note The second "g" in "suggest" is pronounced like the "j" in "jet."

The teachers are quick to suggest
That we study quite hard for a test.
  It takes lots of thought
  To learn what we're taught.
But I think I prefer just to rest.

Concentrating on sibilants

A

Sibilants

Sibilants are sounds that make a hiss or buzz.

Voiced	**Z** (buz**z**)	**ZH** (mea**s**ure)	**J** (**judg**e)
Unvoiced	**S** (bu**s**)	**SH** (wa**sh**)	**CH** (wa**tch**).

1 *Silently* experiment with alternating the unvoiced sounds of **S** and **SH**.

For **S**:

- Press the sides of the tongue against the teeth so that a valley is formed down the center of the tongue.

- If you blow strongly, the air will rush through this narrow valley and make a high hissing noise as it goes past your front teeth: "Sssss."

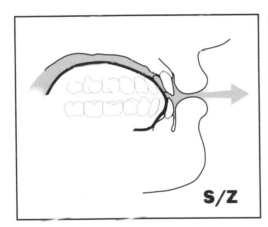 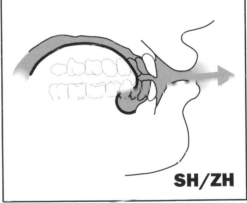

For **SH**:

After saying **S** several times, silently and aloud, move your tongue back just a little. Now there is more room for air to get out.

Slide back and forth between the **S** and the **SH** positions several times, at first silently, then aloud. If you blow out strongly, the sound for **S** will be a higher hiss, and the sound for **SH** will be a lower hiss. If you round your lips for **SH**, the difference will be more clear.

2 Now try both positions *with voicing*. The sounds will now be **Z** and **ZH**.

3 Practice saying these words.

Unvoiced S/SH				Voiced Z/ZH	
Beginning sound		**Final sound**		**Beginning sound**	**Middle sound**
Sue	shoe	mass	mash	zoo	measure
see	she	gas	gash	"z"	pleasure
		mess	mesh		treasure

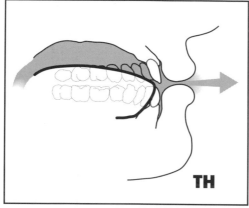

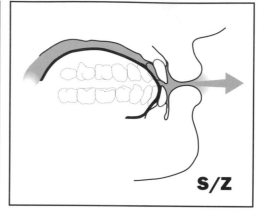

TH is not a sibilant because the tongue is flat and relaxed, so there is no hiss. **S** makes a hiss because the air is forced through a narrow valley.

Unvoiced TH/S				Voiced TH/Z			
Beginning sound		**Final sound**		**Beginning sound**		**Final sound**	
think	sink	math	mass	then	Zen	breathe	breeze
thank	sank	faith	face			clothe	close
thick	sick	mouth	mouse			bathe	bays

B

Sentences using S, SH, and TH (tongue twisters)

Practice saying these sentences out loud.

1. She is certain to show you the sailors from the ship.
2. She sells seashells by the seashore.
3. Miss Beth Smith saw a mouse in the path.

For further work on **TH/S**, see Appendix B.

C
SH/CH *and* J/Y

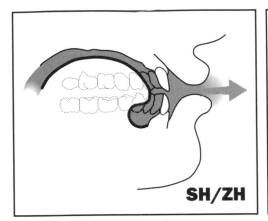

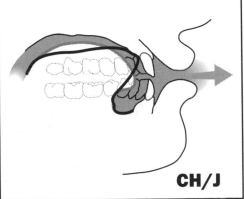

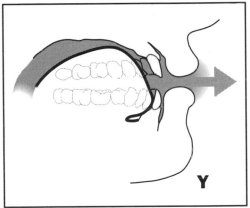

CH is pronounced as a combination of the stop **T**, followed by the continuant **SH**.
Practice these examples.

Unvoiced beginning sounds		Unvoiced final sounds	
SH	**CH**	**SH**	**CH**
share	chair	wish	witch
shoe	chew	dish	ditch
sheep	cheap	mush	much
shop	chop	cash	catch

J is pronounced as a combination of the stop **D**, followed by the continuant **ZH**. Practice these examples.

Joe	joy	just	juice
jar	jury	job	jump
judge	jam	Jack	jelly

Y is pronounced as a continuant. Practice these examples.

yes	young	year	yard
you	your	yet	yellow

Now practice the contrast between these sounds.

Jell-o	yellow	jet	yet
jell	yell	jail	Yale

New York   jam and jelly jars

jumbo jet

D

Pair practice: SH/CH and J/Y

Student 1 says sentence (a) or (b). Student 2 says the answer.

1. a. What did you watch?   A movie.
   b. What did you wash?   My car.

2. a. What does "chatter" mean?   To talk fast.
   b. What does "shatter" mean?   To break glass.

3. a. Does Jack eat much?   No, not a lot.
   b. Does Jack eat mush?   It's his favorite cereal.

4. a. What's a "chip"?   A small piece.
   b. What's a "ship"?   A big boat.
   c. What's a "sip"?   A little drink.

5. a. What does "cheap" mean?   Not expensive.
   b. What does "jeep" mean?   A car for rough roads.

6. a. Where does "c" go in the alphabet?   It's the third letter.
   b. Where does "z" go in the alphabet?   At the end.
   c. Where does "g" go in the alphabet?   In the middle.

7. a. What does "choke" mean?   To strangle.
   b. What does "joke" mean?   A funny story.
   c. What does "yolk" mean?   The yellow part of an egg.

8. a. Her son went to Yale.   That's wonderful!
   b. Her son went to jail.   That's terrible!

9. a. What's Jell-o?   A dessert.
    b. What's yellow?   A color.

10. a. What does "jell" mean?   To become solid.
    b. What does "yell" mean?   To shout.

11. a. How do you spell "jewel"?   J E W E L
    b. How do you spell "you'll"?   Y O U apostrophe L L

E

Sibilants and number of syllables:
S, Z, SH, CH, and J

1 Listen to the following words that end in "-es." In some of these words the "-es" is an extra syllable, and in some it is not.

Note The letter "x" is pronounced "eks," so it ends in a sibilant.

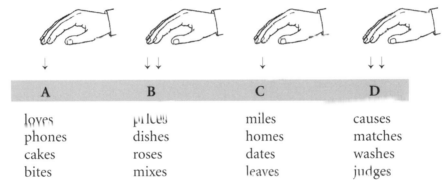

A	B	C	D
loves	prices	miles	causes
phones	dishes	homes	matches
cakes	roses	dates	washes
bites	mixes	leaves	judges

2 Circle the words that have a hissing or buzzing sound before the "-es" ending. There are eight of these words. Can you make a rule for when the "-es" ending is an extra syllable?

F

Pair practice

Student 1 says a word from list 1 or list 2. Student 2 says the other word in the pair.

Example Student 1: roses
           Student 2: rose

Note If a word in list 1 ends in a sibilant (a hissing sound like **SH** or **S**), the "-es" ending in list 2 is pronounced as an extra syllable.

1	2	1	2
rose	roses	wash	washes
ice	ices	cause	causes
dish	dishes	buzz	buzzes
watch	watches	mix	mixes
box	boxes	surprise	surprises
tax	taxes	quiz	quizzes
wax	waxes	rich	riches
badge	badges	judge	judges
rage	rages	page	pages

G

Pair practice: singular or plural?

Student 1 says the singular or plural form of the sentence. Student 2 says the other form of the sentence.

Example Student 1: The match fell on the floor.
  Student 2: The matches fell on the floor.

1. The match (matches) fell on the floor.
2. Did you see the prize (prizes)?
3. What excuse (excuses) did he make?
4. Are there any people on the beach (beaches)?
5. Did you pay the tax (taxes)?
6. Where did you put the box (boxes)?
7. It depends on the price (prices).
8. The rabbit is in the bush (bushes).
9. Did you wash the dish (dishes)?
10. I put the rose (roses) in the vase.

H

Dialogue

Practice the following dialogue with a partner. Pay attention to the number of syllables in these words.

Words ending in sibilants:	surprise/surprises	prize/prizes
	quiz/quizzes	watch/watches
	tax/taxes	
Past tense of words ending in **D** *or* **T**:	decided	

Prizes

A: Do you like surprises?
B: Sometimes. What is it?
A: We have a chance to win some great prizes.
B: How? Go on a TV quiz show?
A: You guessed it! I decided it would be fun.
B: I'm no good at quizzes.
A: But the second prize is a new watch!
B: I don't need any more watches.
A: And the first prize is a million dollars!
B: That's not so great. You have to pay taxes on prize money.

Dictation

1. _____
2. _____
3. _____
4. _____
5. _____

Linking: the same sound

Rule When you link two sounds that are the same, do not say the sound twice. Say the sound once, but make it longer.

1. wash shells	5. all leather	9. team members
2. bus system	6. will loan	10. have vitamins
3. his zoo	7. we're ready	11. half full
4. tax saving	8. far river	12. plan nothing

Now practice linking the same sound in sentences.

13. Sam might go.	16. Bill loves pie.
14. The sun never sets.	17. We both think it's good.
15. I have very good ideas.	18. I wish she'd come.

K
Check yourself

Record these sentences. Listen to yourself. Did you say the right number of syllables?

> Can I have six oranges and two pieces of cheese?... Oh... And three boxes of dates, please. One large and two small.

(Did you have three syllables for "oranges," two for "pieces" and "boxes," and one for "dates" and "small"?)

Review
Number of syllables

For a special challenge, try this exercise. Student 1 says sentence (a) or (b). Student 2 answers.

1. a. How do you spell "please"?   P L E A S E
    b. How do you spell "police"?   P O L I C E

2. a. What kind of train is it?   Passenger.
    b. What kind of terrain is it?   Flat.
        (terrain = landscape)

3. a. What does "furry" mean?   With a lot of fur. (fur = animal hair)
    b. What does "free" mean?   It doesn't cost anything.

4. a. How do you spell "forest"?   F O R E S T
    b. How do you spell "first"?   F I R S T

5. a. What does "squeeze" mean?   To push together.
    b. What does "excuse" mean?   To forgive.

6. a. What's a "clone"?   A copy.
    b. What's a "cologne"?   A weak perfume.

7. a. What does "tense" mean?   Not relaxed.
    b. What does "tennis" mean?   A sport.

8. a. How do you spell "sport"?   S P O R T
    b. How do you spell "support"?   S U P P O R T

7 Rhythm: voicing and syllable length

The end of a word is important in English. Sometimes it is hard to hear the final consonant, so we have an extra signal to help the listener.

Rule If the final sound is voiced, the vowel before it is long.

rise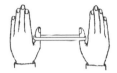

If the final sound is unvoiced, the vowel before it is short.

rice

A
Pair practice

Student 1 says a word from from list 1 or list 2. Student 2 says the other word in the pair.

1 Shorter vowel Unvoiced final consonant	2 Longer vowel Voiced final consonant
safe	save
leaf	leave
half	have
peace	peas
bus	buzz
Miss	Ms.
back	bag
cap	cab
feet	feed
batch	badge
rich	ridge

B

Listening practice 🔳

Listen to a list of three words. Mark a check for the word that is different.

A	B	C

Example You hear: save   save   safe

               ✓

A	B	C

1. have   have ✓ half
2. keep   keep ✓ keys
3. ✓ leaf/lv   lv
4. save ✓ save
5. batch   batch ✓ badge
6. miss ✓ ms   ms
7. cap   cap ✓ cab
8. back ✓ bag   back

C

Pair practice

Student 1 says sentence (a) or (b). Student 2 says the correct answer.

1. a. He wants peas.   Not carrots?
   b. He wants peace.   Not war?

2. a. There's something in my eyes!   Call a doctor!
   b. There's something in my ice!   Call a waiter.

3. a. What does "seize" mean?   To capture.
   b. What does "cease" mean?   To stop.

4. a. Isn't this a good prize?   Yes, did you win it?
   b. Isn't this a good price?   Yes, it's really cheap.

5. a. How do you spell "trace"?   T R A C E
   b. How do you spell "trays"?   T R A Y S

6. a. Lies are terrible.   Yes, the truth is better.
   b. Lice are terrible.   Awful bugs!

7. a. How did you like the plays?   They were great!
   b. How did you like the place?   It was beautiful!

8. a. What does "Miss" mean?   An unmarried woman.
   b. What does "Ms." mean?   A woman.

D

Pair practice: grammar

Student 1 says a word from the verbs list or the nouns list. Student 2 says the other word in the pair.

Note The verb often has a longer final syllable than the noun.

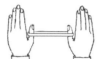 

Verbs	Nouns	Verbs	Nouns
use	use	advise	advice
prove	proof	believe	belief
save	safe	devise	device
teethe	teeth	relieve	relief
excuse	excuse		

E

Pair practice: sentences

Student 1 says the underlined word from sentence (a) or (b). Student 2 says the sentence that fits that word.

Example Student 1: proof
    Student 2: Bring proof tomorrow.

1. a. Can you <u>prove</u> it?
    b. Bring <u>proof</u> tomorrow.

2. a. Good <u>advice</u> is worth gold.
    b. I <u>advise</u> you not to go.

3. a. How long does a baby <u>teethe</u>?
    b. How many <u>teeth</u> does a baby have?

4. a. I <u>believe</u> you.
    b. "<u>Belief</u>" means "faith."

5. a. What <u>excuse</u> did they give?
    b. <u>Excuse</u> me.

6. a. I want to <u>save</u> money.
    b. Is your money <u>safe</u> there?

F

Pair practice: dialogue

1 Practice saying these phrases. Be careful to add length to the syllables that end in voiced sounds.

Voiced	Unvoiced
my eyes	piece of bread crust
tears	it's no use!
close your eyes	of course
is that wise?	

Mixed voiced (V) and unvoiced (UV)

V   UV   UV
use the ice from your glass

2 Now practice this dialogue with a partner.

Trouble at the Restaurant

A: What's the matter?
B: There's something in my eyes.
A: Wash it out with tears.
B: No, it's no use! I think it's a piece of bread crust.
A: Close your eyes and put some ice over them.
B: Is that wise?
A: Of course! Here – use the ice from your glass.

then they do it

G

Words that end in stops

North Americans (both U.S. and Canada) generally do not pronounce final stop sounds completely. For that reason, it is particularly important to notice the length of the vowel sound. A longer vowel means that the word ends in a *voiced* stop.

Practice these words.

Unvoiced	Voiced	Unvoiced	Voiced	Unvoiced	Voiced
bet	bed	back	bag	cap	cab
sat	sad	rack	rag	mop	mob
debt	dead	sack	sag	rope	robe
feet	feed	pick	pig	lap	lab
right	ride	duck	dug	tap	tab

H
Pair practice

Student 1 says sentence (a) or (b). Student 2 says the answer.

1. a. What's a cap?   A kind of hat.
    b. What's a cab?   A taxi.

2. a. What's a buck?   A dollar.
    b. What's a bug?   An insect.

3. a. What's a seat?   Something to sit on.
    b. What's a seed?   Something to plant.

4. a. How do you spell "tight"?   T I G H T
    b. How do you spell "tide"?   T I D E

5. a. What does "wrote" mean?   The past of "write."
    b. What does "rode" mean?   The past of "ride."

6. a. What's a rope for?   To tie up something.
    b. What's a robe for?   To keep you warm.

7. a. What's a lap for?   Your napkin.
    b. What's a lab for?   Research.

8. a. Where's the tack?   On the bulletin board.
    b. Where's the tag?   On the suitcase.

9. a. What does "bright" mean?   The opposite of dark.
    b. What does "bride" mean?   A woman getting married.

10. a. What does "bake" mean?   To cook in the oven.
    b. What does "beg" mean?   To ask for money.

I
Map game: "Oldtimer and Newcomer"

1 First practice street names. Student 1 says the name of a street on the map on page 51. Student 2 points to that street.

2 Then practice these useful phrases:

It's on the northeast corner of Race and Main.

It's in the middle of the block, between Tap and Luff.

It's two blocks north of Pays Drive.

What's the nearest cross street?

Did you say "Tap Alley"?

Do you mean Tab or Tap?

3 Each student must have a copy of the map on page 51. To play the game, the Oldtimers look at the map and list of shops and decide on a location for each shop listed. Then the Oldtimers write the number of all the shops on the map with a pencil.

The Newcomers look at their maps and ask the Oldtimers where the different shops are. Then the Newcomers mark their maps with the number of each shop.

Example   Newcomer: Could you please tell me where the bakery is?
Oldtimer: Sure. It's on the corner of Race Drive and Gray's Alley.
Newcomer: Did you say Grace Alley?
Oldtimer: No, Gray's Alley.
Newcomer: Oh, I see. And I also need to know where the drugstore is.

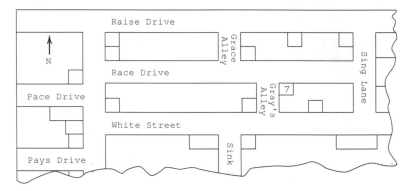

Note   The Oldtimer uses *words only* to tell the locations. No pointing!

4 Check with your partner. Did the Newcomer mark all the right places? Then erase the numbers and change roles.

J
Dictation 📼

1. _____
2. _____
3. _____
4. _____
5. _____

K
Check your progress

Record the dialogue "Trouble at the Restaurant" in Exercise F. Did you lengthen the words that end with voiced sounds?

"Oldtimer and Newcomer"

1. drugstore/pharmacy
2. record store (music store)
3. frozen yogurt shop
4. stationers (office supplies)
5. supermarket
6. hardware store
7. bakery
8. pet store
9. auto supplies store
10. shoe repair shop

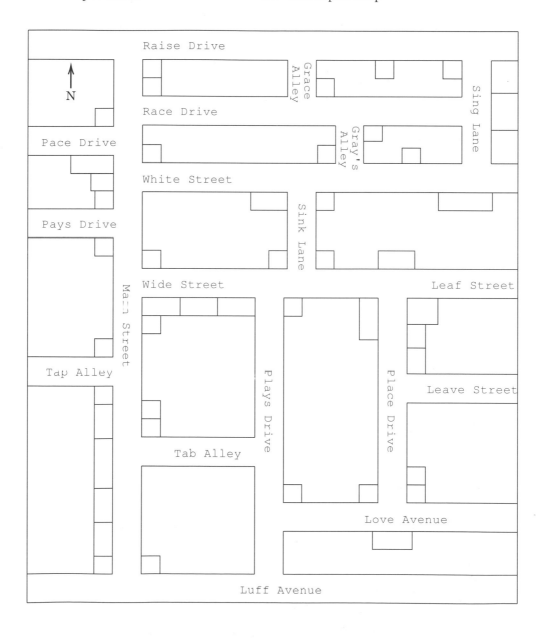

L

Summary: stops/continuants, voiced and unvoiced

	Stops			Continuants					Combination sounds
Unvoiced	P	T	K	S	F	TH	SH	H	CH
Voiced	B	D	G	Z	V	TH	ZH		J

M N L R
all vowels, Y W

Review
Linking

Make new words by linking. Practice linking these sounds. Say each sentence several times until you can hear how the last word sounds like a new word.

1. **R**   We don't fear ice.   rice
2. **B**   They plan to rob us.   bus
3. **SH**   Wash out the dirt.   shout
4. **J**   How much does the judge owe?   Joe
5. **CH**   You can't catch air.   chair

Review
Number of syllables

- Verbs ending in **T** or **D** have an extra syllable in the past tense.
- Words ending in sibilants (**S, Z, SH, ZH, CH, J**) have an extra syllable in the plural or third person singular(he/she/it).

Practice saying the following words. Write the number of syllables after each word.

Past tense	Number of Syllables	Past tense	Number of Syllables
started	____	saved	____
rented	____	hoped	____
recorded	____	planned	____
completed	____	judged	____
stopped	____	lifted	____

Plural or third person singular	Number of Syllables		Plural or third person singular	Number of Syllables
ices	_____		fences	_____
juices	_____		completes	_____
uses	_____		trades	_____
judges	_____		mixes	_____
sentences	_____		manages	_____
pleases	_____		freezes	_____
loves	_____		saves	_____
believes	_____		attaches	_____
parades	_____		colleges	_____

Stress: vowel length

Contrast makes some things easier to see than others.

---

ba**na**na   **Ca**nada

You have practiced the difference between "me"/"meat" and "eyes"/"ice."
The difference in vowel length is a **contrast**. It helps the listener recognize the
final sounds.

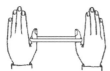

me	meat
eyes	ice

An even more important difference in syllable length is the contrast between stressed
and unstressed syllables.

Listen to these words:

banana	Canada	Alabama
• — •	— • •	— • — •

Rule 1 In every English word with more than one syllable, one syllable is stressed
the most.

Examples **pi**zza   **co**medy
lemon   com**mit**tee
rented

Rule 2 Stressed vowels are extra long.

Rule 3 Most unstressed vowels are reduced (extra short). A reduced vowel is
called *schwa*.

Examples Oklahoma   Arizona   Manitoba
— • — •   — • — •   • — • •

54

A

Stressed syllables: rhythm

In the following words, the stressed syllables are in bold letters. Practice saying these words, making a contrast between the long stressed syllables and the short unstressed syllables.

— •	• —	• — •	— • •
sofa	a**round**	so**lu**tion	**beau**tiful
oven	e**vent**	ar**range**ment	**hor**rible
picture	ar**range**	it's **aw**ful	**o**pen it

B

Full and reduced vowels: rhythm

Because the schwa (reduced vowel) is short, it affects the rhythm of the syllables. A sentence made of words with all full (unreduced) vowels is unusual and sounds very emphatic.

Example (a newspaper headline) ZOO SNAKE BITES MAN

 Listen to these sentences. Some of them have full vowels, and some have a mixture of full and reduced vowels. Tap out the rhythm on your desk to help you concentrate. Whisper the sentences (speak without voicing) so that you can hear the rhythm better.

1. a. Sam likes plain soap.   (all full length vowels)
   b. Mister Johnson likes expensive soap.   (full and schwa mixed)

2. a. Don't feed bears.   (sign at the zoo)
   b. We never feed the bears.

3. a. Zoo snake bites man.   (newspaper headline)
   b. The snake was terrified.

4. a. Maintain airport runways.
   b. The workers are repairing the road.

C

Listening for full and reduced vowels

Listen to ten sentences. Do you only hear full vowels, or is there a mixture of full and schwa vowels? Mark a check in the correct column.

Examples

	All full vowels	A mixture of full and schwa vowels
Go tell Grace.	✓	
Go and tell it to Grace.		✓

	All full vowels	A mixture of full and schwa vowels
1.		
2.		
3.		
4.		
5.		
6.		
7.		
8.		
9.		
10.		

D

More listening practice

The stressed vowel is always full (lengthened). Other vowels may also be full, but the stressed vowel is the longest. Listen to the following names of places. Underline the stressed vowels. Practice saying the names of these places using English rhythm.

1 full vowel	2 full vowels	3 full vowels
Alaska	New York	San Francisco
Nevada	Chicago	United States
Dallas	Mexico	North Carolina
Nebraska	Manitoba	Acapulco
Canada	Los Angeles	

E

Speaking practice

Practice these words. If you whisper you can hear the contrast in length better.

chocolate	success	cafeteria
service	algebra	telephone
president	minister	application

F

Pair practice: abbreviations

Student 1 chooses any question from the list. Student 2 answers it. Take turns until all the questions are answered.

Note The last letter in an abbreviation usually gets the most stress.

Examples T**V**   BB**C**   US**A**

1. What does TV mean?   television
2. What does UN mean?   United Nations
3. What does DC mean?   District of Columbia (Washington D.C.)

4. What does BC mean?   British Columbia (Canada)
5. What does LA mean?   Los Angeles

6. What does USA mean?   United States of America
7. What does BBC mean?   British Broadcasting Company
8. What does CNN mean?   Cable News Network
9. What does CBC mean?   Canadian Broadcasting Corporation

9 Stress: vowel clarity

A
Vowel clarity 🔲

1 Listen to this word. Which syllable has the full, clear vowel sound?

banana

The word "banana" is written with three letter "a" vowels. But only one "a" is said with a full, clear sound. The other two letter "a" vowels are said with an unclear vowel sound. This is the sound of the reduced vowel, *schwa*. The symbol for schwa is "**ə**".

2 Listen to these words and notice the difference between schwa and the full vowel sounds.

ə ə	ə ə	ə ə	ə ə
Alaska	pajamas	Africa	Oklahoma

Rule All stressed vowels are full and *clear*.

Clear vowels	Unclear vowels (schwa)
full (long)	reduced
can be stressed	cannot be stressed

3 Schwa is the most common vowel sound in spoken English because *any* vowel can be reduced to "unclear."

	ə ə	ə ə	ə ə	ə	ə
Examples	Nebraska	Manitoba	economics	Europe	chocolate

4 Listen to these words. Underline the clear vowels. Practice pronouncing the words.

"ə+r" endings	Noun/adjective	Verb
enter	German	arrange
answer	Swedish	record
dollar	Irish	excuse
sugar	Japanese	advise
shower	American	pronounce
color	African	announce
honor	Spanish	exchange

B

Listening practice: identifying schwa 🔲

Listen to these words. Draw a slash through the unclear vowels (ə). Then practice saying the words.

Examples Canada   banana   basket   open

1 clear vowel	2 clear vowels
problem	mathematics
printed	economics
drama	economy
extra	photography
computer	absolute
employment	application
requirement	international

C

Pair practice: words

Student 1 says a word from list A or list B. Student 2 says the other word in the pair.

Example Student 1: atom
                Student 2: Tom

1.

A Clear vowel	B Clear vowel + unclear vowel
Tom	atom
man	woman
men	women
add	added
face	surface

2.

A Clear + unclear	B Unclear + clear + unclear
office	official
atom	atomic
added	addition

D
Limerick

The syllables in bold letters have clear, long vowels. Listen and practice.

A **stu**dent was **sent** to Ta**co**ma*
In**tend**ing to **earn** a di**plo**ma.
He **said**, "With the **rain**,
I don't **want** to re**main**.
I **think** I'd pre**fer** Okla**ho**ma."**

*Tacoma, Washington, is an especially rainy city.
**Oklahoma is an especially dry state.

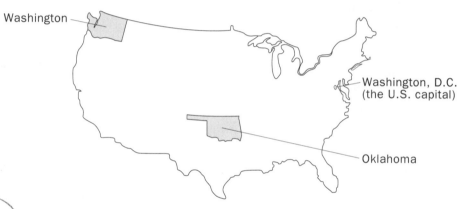

Washington

Washington, D.C.
(the U.S. capital)

Oklahoma

E
Pair practice: **can** and **can't**

You have already practiced the contrast between the stop and continuant endings of "can" and "can't." There is another signal that English speakers use to contrast these words.

Rule "Can't" is usually said with a full clear vowel. "Can" is usually said with a schwa.

> *Example* We can do it.
> They can't do it.

Student 1 says sentence (a) or (b). Student 2 answers.

1. a. I can go. Oh, good.
   b. I can't go. That's too bad!

2. a. She can do it. That's fine.
   b. She can't do it. She should try harder.

3. a. Where can we go? Any tourist destination.
   b. Where can't we go? Into the military zone.

4. a. We can leave now. Good, I'll get my things.
   b. We can't leave now. All right, we'll wait.

5. a. Can you do this? Of course.
   b. Can't you do this? No, I can't.

6. a. Why can you do that? Because I have permission.
   b. Why can't you do that? Because I don't know how.

7. a. Can a cat fly? No.
   b. Can't a cat fly? Are you crazy?

8. a. What can we do? Make an effort.
   b. What can't we do? Fly without an airplane.

9. a. Can you type? Yes, of course.
   b. Can't you type? Unfortunately, no.

10. a. When can you come? Right away.
    b. When can't you come? When I'm too busy.

F

Word rhythm/sentence rhythm 🔲

A single word has its own rhythm pattern. This pattern can be just like the rhythm pattern of a sentence. Listen and then draw dots and dashes under the following pairs.

1. at**trac**tive   It's **active**.
   • —— •   • —— •

2. absolute   Have some fruit.

3. responsible   It's possible.

4. electrification   I need a vacation.

5. scientific   I'm terrific!

6. photography   It's hard for me.

7. economic   It's atomic.

8. institution   End pollution.

9. pronunciation   Let's tell the nation.

G
Check your progress: dialogue

Circle the stressed syllable in the underlined words. Then practice saying the dialogue. Record the dialogue. Did you give extra length to the stressed syllables?

Students

X: What are you <u>studying</u>?

Y: Economics. What about you?

X: <u>Photography</u>.

Y: Then you must take good <u>photographs</u>.

X: And YOU must be good with <u>money</u>!

Review
Final sounds: consonant clusters

Student 1 says one of the underlined words in each pair. Student 2 says the sentence using that word.

Example   Student 1: criticisms
Student 2: I didn't like the criticisms I was hearing.

1. a. I didn't like the <u>criticism</u> Albert gave.
   b. I didn't like the <u>criticisms</u> I was hearing.

2. a. They <u>like</u> all the food.
   b. They <u>liked</u> everything.

3. a. Did you like the <u>present</u> Alice brought?
   b. Did you like the <u>presents</u> Alice gave you?

4. a. The laboratory is testing for <u>salt</u> in the food.
   b. The laboratory is testing for <u>salts</u> in the water.

5. a. The horses <u>pull</u> all the carts.
   b. The horses <u>pulled</u> every cart.

6. a. The <u>car</u> is ready.
   b. The <u>cart</u> is missing.

10 Word stress patterns

A
Stress patterns

Listen to the following words. Notice the stress pattern.

President **Lin**coln

Prime Minister Mac**don**ald

Rule Using the correct stress pattern is more important than using the correct sounds.

Listen to the following words. Underline the syllable with the strongest stress.

hamburger	extremely	refrigerate
cookies	accurate	refrigerator
pizza	machine	refrigeration

B
Two-syllable names and phrases

Rule If you leave out verbs, 90 percent of two-syllable words are stressed on the first syllable.

Two-syllable personal names are also likely to be stressed on the first syllable.

Listen and practice saying these names and phrases.

Charlie Chaplin	instant coffee
Jodie Foster	chocolate candy
Judy Garland	English muffin
Michael Jackson	frozen yogurt
Peter Jennings	
Dolly Parton	
Elvis Presley	
Robert Redford	

Can you think of other two-syllable names and phrases?

C
Stress pattern rules 🔲

Rule 1 In every word with *two* syllables, one vowel will be stressed (long and clear). The other vowel is usually schwa.

Example **fro**zen **yo**gurt
— • — •

Rule 2 In words with *three or more* syllables:

- One vowel will get the main stress (long and clear).
- Some vowels may get a little stress (clear, but not as long as the vowel with the most stress).
- Some vowels may be reduced (schwa).

Examples eco**no**mic   **ar**gument
• • — •   — • •

calculator   adminis**tra**tion
— • — •   • — • — •

Practice the rhythm of the following words.

3 syllables	4 syllables	5 syllables	6 syllables
re**duc**tion	oppo**si**tion	partici**pa**tion	identifi**ca**tion
sug**ges**tion	compli**ca**tion	exami**na**tion	electrifi**ca**tion
in**ten**tion	regis**tra**tion	adminis**tra**tion	
per**mis**sion	poli**ti**cian	contami**na**tion	

D
Patterns

1 Underline the *main* stress in the following words.

collection	information	simplification
relation	calculation	
precision	operation	
addition	estimation	
permission	medication	
reaction	separation	
decision	distribution	

Pattern In words ending in "tion" or "sion," the stress is in the next to last syllable.

2 Where is the vowel with the main stress in the following words? Can you make a rule about this?

static	Atlantic	robotic
comic	terrific	aerobic
electric	narcotic	strategic
economic	Pacific	photographic
domestic	statistic	diplomatic

3 Where is the vowel with the main stress in list A below? In list B?

A	B
economical	economy
technological	technology
surgical	surgery
comical	comedy
chemical	chemistry
political	policy
	equality

Answers

2. The main stress comes before "ic."
3. A The main stress comes before "ical."
    B The main stress comes before "omy," "ogy," "ery," "edy," "istry," and "ity."

E

Pronouncing two clear vowels together

Some words have two clear vowels together. One of the clear vowels is stressed, so it is longer. Practice these words.

bi**o**logy	tr**i**angle	re**a**ction	re**a**lity	ge**o**graphy
ge**o**logy	cre**a**tion	recre**a**tion	science	associ**a**tion

F

Linking two vowels together: "e" and "y"/ "o"and "ow"

Rule 1 When the letters "e" or "y" link with a vowel, the linking sound is like the first sound of "yes."

> *Examples*   We‿agree.   Say‿it.
>   y   y

Rule 2 When "o" or "ow" link with a vowel, the linking sound is like the first sound of "way."

Examples   Go͜ on.   How͜ about it?
　　　　　　　w　　　　　w

G

Linking vowels ("y" and "w"): stories

1 Draw linking marks for the underlined words that follow. Use the **y** sound or the **w** sound to link the two words.

2 Then read the stories out loud, saying the linked words as one word.

At the Beach

[1]We often go to the beach on the weekend. [2]We always go by car, because it's fastest. [3]My roomate will try anything. [4]He loves to surf, but he isn't a great surfer. [5]He always falls off the surfboard. [6]"What's the answer?" he asked me. [7]"I hate to say it, but I think you should find another sport," I answered.

Jokes Between Friends

[1]Sometimes I go over to my friend's house. [2]The first thing she says is "How are you?" [3]If I really tell her how I am, she doesn't listen. [4]This happens so often that I decided to answer "fine" every time. [5]But then I said, "You always ask, but you don't listen." [6]So she apologized and said, "From now on I'll do better." [7]Then she asked, "How are you?" and I said "Terrible!" [8]She knew I was joking, so she said, "That's great! See how I'm listening to everything you say?"

66

Grammar 🔲

1 Listen to the following words. Which syllable gets the main stress?

Noun	Verb
record	record
object	object
permit	permit
suspect	suspect
conflict	conflict
contract	contract

Rule In verbs with two syllables, the main stress is often on the second syllable. (Except for verbs, 90 percent of two-syllable words are stressed on the first syllable.)

2 "Two-word verbs" (phrasal verbs) are very common in English. Notice the pattern for nouns and verbs.

Noun	Verb
a **set**up (an arrangement)	to set **up** (to arrange)
an **up**set (a disturbance)	to up**set** (to disturb)
a **hold**up (a robbery)	to hold **up** (to stop something)
a **look**out (a person who watches)	to look **out** (to be careful)
a **try**out (a test, an audition)	to try **out** (to test something or someone)
checkout (a place to check out)	to check **out** (to pay a bill and leave)
a **turn**around (a place to turn around)	to turn **around** (to go the other way)
a **turn**off (something you do not like)	to turn **off** (to displease)

I

Pair practice

Student 1 says either the noun form or the verb form of each pair of underlined words. Student 2 says the sentence that matches the word you hear.

  1. a. Let's make a <u>record</u> of that song.
      b. Let's <u>record</u> that song.

2. a. What's this little object?
    b. We object to that.

3. a. They suspect him of a crime.
    b. That's the suspect.

4. a. We gave her a present.
    b. They plan to present an award.

5. a. The author wants to contrast good and evil.
    b. There is a contrast between dark and light.

6. a. It was a terrible conflict.
    b. His views conflict with mine.

7. a. They agreed to sign a contract.
    b. Cold air makes metal contract.

8. a. Did you set up the display?
    b. This is a great setup!

9. a. The thief sent a lookout to watch for the police.
    b. You'd better look out or you'll have an accident!

10. a. This is a holdup! Give me your money!
    b. The train is going to hold up traffic.

J

Combined words

English often combines words to make a new word. These combinations are pronounced as a single noun, with the stress on the first syllable.

Example "house" + "boat" makes "houseboat"

Note Sometimes combined words are written as one word and sometimes as two words. Check your dictionary.

Practice these combined words:

houseboat	**rain**coat	**dri**ver's seat
light bulb	**shoe**box	**bas**ketball
phone book	**pass**port	**vo**lleyball
hot dog	**book**store	**base**ball
bathroom	**air**line	**post** office
dishwasher	**park**way	**cof**fee pot
high school	**Sup**er Burger	
speed limit	**fo**cus words	

K
Pair practice

Read the following sentences. Then challenge your partner. Student 1 says sentence (a) or (b). Student 2 answers.

Note If you say words using their correct stress pattern, it is easier for other people to understand you, even if you do not get the sounds exactly right.

1. a. What did you think of the com**mit**tee? They're writing a good report.
   b. What did you think of the **co**medy? It wasn't very funny.

2. a. What does "**el**igible" mean? Qualified.
   b. What does "il**leg**ible" mean? Unreadable.

3. a. Does she want a **nee**dle? Yes, she wants to sew on a new button.
   b. Does she want **an**y doll? No, she needs a special one.

4. a. What does "**es**timator" mean? A person who figures costs.
   b. What does "a **steam** motor" mean? There's no such thing!

5. a. Do the students like **his**tory? No, too many dates.
   b. Do the students like his **sto**ry? Yes, it's funny.

6. a. How do you spell "**de**puty"? D E P U T Y
   b. How do you spell "the **beau**ty"? As two words.

7. a. Is it ele**men**tary? No, it's advanced.
   b. Is it a **le**mon tree? No, an orange tree.

8. a. What's for **rain**? An umbrella.
   b. What's **for**eign? Another language.

9. a. Is that **Eu**rope? No, it's China.
   b. Is that your **rope**? No, it's hers.

10. a. What's in the **des**ert? Sand.
    b. What's in the des**sert**? Sugar.

L
Check yourself

1 Look at the underlined words in the dialogue on page 70. Circle the syllables with the main stress.

2 Then practice saying the dialogue, making the stressed syllables longer.

3 Record the dialogue if you can. Did you lengthen the syllables you had circled?

Conversation on a Train

(Two commuters, on their way to work in the city, are talking.)

First Commuter: What <u>business</u> are you in?

Second Commuter: <u>Photography</u>.

First Commuter: Oh yeah? <u>Interesting</u>. Is there a lot of <u>money</u> in it?

Second Commuter: Well, you have to <u>look out</u> for expenses. They can <u>eat up</u> your profit.

First Commuter: Eat it up? And how much money do you need to <u>set up</u> a business like that?

Second Commuter: Oh, a lot! The <u>setup</u> is <u>expensive</u> – <u>chemicals</u>, <u>photographic</u> equipment. Lots of stuff.

First Commuter: I see. Well, maybe I'll just stick to my present <u>occupation</u>.

Review

Number of syllables

Write the past tense of the regulat verbs below. How many syllables are there in the past tense?

	Past tense	Number of syllables
1. serve	_____	_____
2. perform	_____	_____
3. protect	_____	_____
4. burn	_____	_____
5. disturb	_____	_____
6. arrange	_____	_____
7. jump	_____	_____
8. pretend	_____	_____

Review

Linking

Practice linking these common expressions.

1. Look out!
2. Watch out!
3. Hurry up!
4. How are you?
5. How's it going?

6. What's new?
7. What's up?
8. Come on!
9. It's about time!
10. How about that!

11 Basic Emphasis Pattern: content words

The butterfly on the right is easier to see because it is highlighted (emphasized) and everything else is in the shade (de-emphasized).

English speakers use a basic pattern of emphasis. If you use this pattern, you will

- Hear better.
- Be understood better.

Rule In English, the content words are usually emphasized. **Content words** are words that have the most information in a sentence.

Basic Emphasis Pattern			
Content words (emphasized)	*nouns* (cat)	*main verbs* (runs)	*adverbs* (quickly)	*adjectives* (happy)
	question words (who, what, where, when, why, how)			
Structure words* (de-emphasized)	*pronouns* (he, she)	*prepositions* (of, to, at)	*articles* (a, the)	*"to be" verbs* (is, was)
	conjunctions (and, but)	*auxiliary verbs* (can, have, do, will)		

* Structure words will be discussed in Unit 12.

The content words are easier to hear because they are given extra emphasis. Words are emphasized by adding extra length to their stressed syllables.

The type of word listed below is underlined in the sentences.

Examples

1.	(noun)	This is my <u>cat</u>.
2.	(main verb)	What does it <u>eat</u>?
3.	(adverb)	Please come <u>quickly</u>.
4.	(adjective)	You did <u>excellent</u> work.
5.	(question word)	<u>Why</u> did you write the letter?

A
Pair practice

With a partner, write content words that fit these categories.

Nouns	Verbs	Adverbs	Adjectives	Question words
car	run	quickly	red	what
office	talk	happily	hot	where

B
Locating content words

Circle the content words in the following sentences. Compare your circled words with another student.

Example My (cat) (eats) (fish) and she (likes) to (hunt) (mice) in the (garden).

1. Do you like the picture on your passport?
2. Did you take a test for a driver's license in this country?
3. University students pay a lot of money for their books.
4. High school students get their books free.
5. Do you think it is harder to speak or to hear a new language?
6. Is there a speed limit for cars in your country?

C
Emphasizing content words 🔘▭

Practice saying the following sentences. Make the stressed syllables long. That makes it easy to hear the content words.

1. He rented an apartment.
2. The professor is famous.
3. The painter is coming.
4. She's written the report.
5. It's difficult to understand.
6. He's planning to retire.

D
Limerick

Note You have practiced the rhythm of this limerick in Unit 9, Exercise D. Now say it again and notice which words are emphasized.

One good way to practice the following limerick is by whispering instead of speaking. Whispering will help you concentrate better on emphasizing the content words.

> A student was sent to Tacoma
> Intending to earn a diploma.
> He said, "With the rain,
> I don't want to remain.
> I think I'd prefer Oklahoma."

E
Group work: telegrams

Today, when people are in a hurry to get a message to someone, they use the telephone or a fax machine. But in the old days, people sent telegrams. Because the sender of the telegram had to pay for each word, it was cheaper to use only content words.

Example SEND MONEY. BOUGHT CAR.
　　　　　This means "Send me money. I've bought a car."

1 Read the long message below these instructions.

2 Write this message as a telegram. Which words can you cut? Which words do you need in order to keep the meaning? Discuss this with your group.

3 Write the shortest message possible.

Phone Message

The book that you ordered has arrived in the bookstore. Our address is 921 Main Street. The store is open from 10 to 6 every day of the week except Sunday. Your book will be kept for you at the customer service counter at the front of the store.

F
Pair work: telegrams

1 Write a telegram with your own message. Use only content words.

2 Exchange your telegram with a partner. Can you fill in the structure words in your partner's telegram?

G
Dialogue 🔲

1 Circle the content words in the following dialogue. You should find eight.

2 Practice the dialogue, lengthening the stressed syllables of the content words.

Lost Glasses

A: What's the matter?
B: I lost my glasses.
A: Where'd you put them?
B: If I knew, I could find them!

H
Note taking 🔲

1 Listen to this story.

2 Listen again and write only the words you hear most clearly. Leave blanks for the words that are not very clear.

3 Fill in the blanks by guessing the missing words.

4 Listen again and see if you guessed the right meaning.

Note Even if all the words you guessed aren't exactly the same as those you heard, if the meaning is the same, you have taken notes successfully.

I
Check yourself

1 Practice the different stress patterns in the following words.

Noun	Adjective
content	con**tent**

2 Practice saying this short poem.

> These lines can show you where the accent went.
> But with their [1]content, I'm not yet [2]content.
>   (John Hollander)

Which "content" is used as a noun?

Review

Linking: stop-to-stop

If the final stop is the same sound as the beginning of the next word, say the words as one word.

Example   deep pot   deeppot

1. cab back   put ten   black cat
    deep pot   red door   big gate

2. a. Please stop pushing.

    b. Cook it in a deep pot.

    c. I took a cab back to town.

    d. What's a "lab beaker?"

    e. Put ten dollars in the box.

    f. Is this the right town?

    g. That's a bad dog.

    h. Open the red door.

    i. Our luck could change.

    j. She has a black cat.

12 Basic Emphasis Pattern: structure words

Rule **Structure words** are usually reduced (de-emphasized).

Basic Emphasis Pattern				
Content words (emphasized)	*nouns* (cat)	*main verbs* (runs)	*adverbs* (quickly)	*adjectives* (happy)
	question words (who, what, where, when, why, how)			
Structure words (de-emphasized)	*pronouns* (he, she)	*prepositions* (of, to, at)	*articles* (a, the)	*"to be" verbs* (is, was)
	conjunctions (and, but)	*auxiliary verbs* (can, have, do, will)		

When content words are emphasized and structure words are de-emphasized, the contrast helps the listener to hear the important words.

A
Pair practice

With a partner, write structure words that fit these categories.

Pronouns	Prepositions	Articles*	"To be" verbs	Conjunctions	Auxiliary verbs
he	in	a	is	and	can
ours	at	an	were	but	do
_____	over	the	_____	so	have
_____	_____		_____	or	will
_____	_____		_____		
_____	_____				
_____	_____				

*These are the only articles.

B
Contractions

"To contract" means to make something smaller. Contractions are a normal part of spoken English. Contractions reduce attention to structure words, helping to make the content words easier to notice.

1 Listen to the difference between some typical contractions and their full forms. Notice the change in the number of syllables.

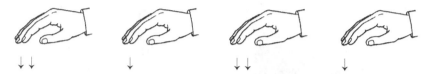

Full form	Contraction	Full form	Contraction
a. I am	I'm	f. he has	he's
b. is not	isn't (2 syllables)	g. I will	I'll
c. they have	they've	h. I have	I've
d. that is	that's	i. we have	we've
e. I would	I'd	j. she had	she'd

2 Practice the following pairs of words. Tap the syllables while you are speaking.

Full form	Contraction	Full form	Contraction
a. she is	she's	f. who is	who's
b. cannot	can't	g. where did	where'd
c. I have	I've	h. we are	we're
d. why have	why've	i. they are	they're
e. he has	he's	j. he had	he'd

C
Pair practice: sentences

Student 1 says sentence (a) or (b) with the contraction. Student 2 says the full word.

1. a. They've already gone.   have
   b. They'd already gone.   had

2. a. How long've you been there?   have
   b. How long'd you been there?   had

3. a. Where'd you put that?   did
   b. Where'll you put that?   will

4. a. It'll cost a lot.   will
    b. It'd cost a lot.   would

5. a. We're shut down completely.   are
    b. We'd shut down completely.   had

6. a. We'd be pleased to help.   would
    b. We'll be pleased to help.   will

7. a. They'll cut the bread.   will
    b. They'd cut the bread.   had
    c. They've cut the bread.   have

8. a. What've you put in the soup?   have
    b. What'll you put in the soup?   will

9. a. Where'd everybody go?   did
    b. Where'll everybody go?   will

10. a. I've run in that race.   have
    b. I'll run in that race   will

D
Reduced **and** 📼

The structure word "and" is one of the most common words in English. "And" is usually contracted to a schwa + "n,"

Practice saying the reduced "and" in order to hear it better. Link the final sound of the first word to the schwa vowel of "and."

1. cream an' sugar
2. sandwich an' coffee
3. big an' little
4. rich an' famous
5. men an' women
6. boys an' girls
7. rock an' roll
8. knives an' forks
9. peanut butter an' jelly
10. hamburger an' fries
11. nickels an' dimes
12. tables an' chairs
13. radio an' television

E

Pair practice: dialogue

1 Reduce "and."

2 Emphasize the content words.

     At the Cafe

A: I'd like a chicken sandwich and coffee.
B: Do you want everything on the sandwich?
A: What's everything?
B: Mustard, mayonnaise, lettuce, tomatoes, and pickles.
A: Everything but the mayonnaise.
B: Cream and sugar with your coffee?
A: No, I like it black. Black and hot.

F

Reduced can

1 Listen to these sentences. The vowel in "can" is reduced, but the vowel in "can't" is full and clear.

John can write very well.
John can't write very well.

2 Now read the following sentences. Underline the clear vowel in "can't." Draw a slash (/) through the reduced vowel in "can."

Then Student 1 says sentence (a) or (b). Student 2 answers.

1. a. John can write very well.   Yes, I agree.
   b. John can't write very well.   That's unfortunate.

2. a. Can you go tonight?   Yes, I finished my work.
   b. Can't you go tonight?   Unfortunately, no.

3. a. The audience can hear the speaker.   That's good.
   b. The audience can't hear the speaker.   That's terrible!

4. a. We can always eat before class.   Yes, I prefer it.
   b. We can't always eat before class.   No, sometimes not.

5. a. Did you say they can come?   Yes, it's possible.
   b. Did you say they can't come?   It's impossible.

6. a. The Johnsons can afford the trip.   Oh, good!
   b. The Johnsons can't afford the trip.   That's too bad.

G
Common expressions ▭

Practice the contractions and reductions in these common friendly greetings and remarks.

1. What's new?
2. How're you doing?
3. How's it going?
4. How've you been?
5. What's up?

6. Who's here?
7. What'll you have?   (to eat or drink)
8. Here's to you!   (a toast)
9. Can I help you?
10. It's been fun!

H
Silent H

Pronouns are usually reduced so much that words like "he," "him," "hers," and "his" lose the beginning sound **H**, except at the beginning of sentences.

Practice saying the following.

Examples

Slow, full	Fast, reduced
Is he?	izzy
give her	giver
Would he?	woody

Is h̶e?

Note Linking is especially important with silent **H**.

Read the following sentences. Cross out (✗) the "h" at the beginning of words in these sentences.

Then Student 1 says sentence (a) or (b). Student 2 answers.

1. a. Did he go?　　　　　No, he didn't.
   b. Did she go?　　　　　No, she didn't.

2. a. Is her work good?　　Yes, she does well.
   b. Is his work good?　　Yes, he does well.

3. a. Give him a message.　He isn't here.
   b. Give her a message.　She isn't here.

4. a. Did you take her pen?　No, it's mine.
   b. Did you take your pen?　No, I left it.
   (*Note* The **Y** sound is important in "your.")

5. a. Is this his apartment?　He lives across the street.
   b. Is this Sue's apartment?　She lives across the street.

81

6. a. Is he busy?   No, he isn't.
   b. Is she busy?   No, she isn't.

7. a. Can he read?   Yes, quite well.
   b. Can't he read?   Unfortunately, no.

I

Pair practice: linking over the H

1 Draw linking marks wherever you see an "h" that should be dropped. There are six.

2 Practice the dialogue.

 The Missing Singer

Stage Manager:	Where's our singer?
Assistant:	I think he's practicing, sir.
Stage Manager:	But we need him on stage <u>now</u>!
Assistant:	Well, you know how nervous he gets.
Stage Manager:	Did you tell him the concert's about to start?
Assistant:	It sounds like he's practicing just as fast as he can.

Remember, it is not necessary for you to use these reductions and contractions in your speech, but it is very important for you to learn to hear them easily.

J

Dictation

1. _____
2. _____
3. _____
4. _____
5. _____

K

Rhythm

There are three pronouns with a silent **H** in the following limerick. Practice linking the words.

A Train Ride

A singer once went to Vancouver,
Thinking the move would improve her.
But the trip was so long,
And her voice grew so strong,
At Toronto they had to remove her.

L

Reduced T: present tense

In verbs like "want to," the "to" is often reduced so much that the **T** sound is silent.

Examples   "want to" sounds like "wanna"
             "going to" sounds like "gonna"

Note Do not use the "sounds like" spelling in your writing. This spelling is used here only to show the sounds of spoken English.

Listen to these sentences and check "Slow, full" or "Fast, reduced."

Examples

	Slow, full	Fast, reduced
a. I want to go.	✓	
b. I "wanna" go.		✓
c. I am going to go.	✓	
d. I'm "gonna" go.		✓

Slow, full	Fast, reduced
1.	
2.	
3.	
4.	
5.	
6.	
7.	
8.	
9.	
10.	

M

Reduced T: past tense

In the past tense, **T** becomes a quick **D** sound or is silent. Notice the difference in the number of syllables between the present tense and past tense of "want to."

Examples

	Fast speech	Present	Past	Number of Syllables
You hear:	I wanna go.	✓		4
	I wanXeda go.		✓	5

How should you write the sentences above?

Answers I want to go.
I wanted to go.

Listen to these sentences and check "present" or "past." ⬛

Present	Past
1.	
2.	
3.	
4.	
5.	

N

Reduced **T** in between vowels

T often sounds like a quick **D** in between vowels. Practice saying **T** this way so that you can recognize it when you listen to an English speaker.

Example "write it" sounds like "ride it"

water	fit any
better	lot of
liter	get all
later	
hotter	write it
city	hit it
Betty	
atom	

Review

Content words

1 Circle the content words.

2 Then practice saying the poem.

I think that I shall never see
  A billboard lovely as a tree.
Indeed unless the billboards fall,
  I'll never see a tree at all.
                    (Ogden Nash)

13 Focus 1: pitch patterns used for emphasis

Conversation

Rule 1 Basic Emphasis Pattern

- Content words are emphasized.
- Structure words are de-emphasized.

Rule 2 Focus

"Focus" means to see clearly. The **focus word** in a sentence has the most emphasis so that the listener can hear it clearly.

Example **Follow that car !**

Rule 3 Melody

We help listeners to notice the focus word (the most important word) by changing the pitch.

The sound of our voice rises on the focus word and then falls. This makes a contrast with less important words. English listeners pay attention to this change in pitch.

Examples   X: Follow that car!

Y: Which car?

A

At the beginning of a conversation

Rule At the beginning of a conversation, the last **content** word is usually the focus of meaning.

Practice humming the melody of the following sentences with the pitch pattern shown. (Humming is singing with "mmmmm" instead of words.) Then practice saying the sentences.

Examples   a. The dog chased a rabbit.

b. What are you doing?

c. I lost my key.

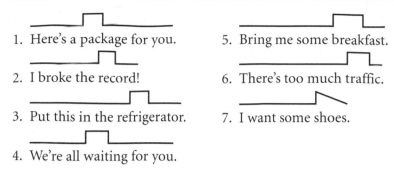

1. Here's a package for you.
2. I broke the record!
3. Put this in the refrigerator.
4. We're all waiting for you.

5. Bring me some breakfast.
6. There's too much traffic.
7. I want some shoes.

B

More practice with focus

1 Find the final content word in each of the following sentences and underline its stressed syllable.

2 Say the sentences, letting your voice rise on the stressed syllable, and then drop after that. This makes the focus clear to the listener.

1. What happened to the electricity?
2. We need a better photograph.
3. He's studying photography.
4. You always need to prepare.
5. The car was sold.
6. You don't understand.
7. He doesn't understand her.
8. Where did you put it?
9. Open the door for them.
10. Please record it for me.

C

After the beginning of a conversation

Rule After a conversation begins, the focus changes as each person speaks, so *any* word can be the focus.

The focus changes because the speaker wants to call attention to **new information**. **Old information** is already understood and does not need emphasis.

1 Practice this dialogue with a partner.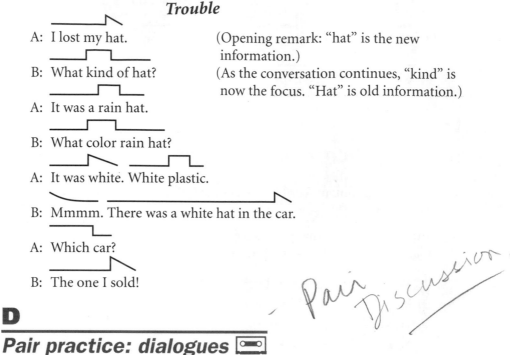

Trouble

A: I lost my hat.　　　　(Opening remark: "hat" is the new
　　　　　　　　　　　　information.)

B: What kind of hat?　　(As the conversation continues, "kind" is
　　　　　　　　　　　　now the focus. "Hat" is old information.)

A: It was a rain hat.

B: What color rain hat?

A: It was white. White plastic.

B: Mmmm. There was a white hat in the car.

A: Which car?

B: The one I sold!

Pair Discussion.

D

Pair practice: dialogues

1 Practice this dialogue using a change in pitch to emphasize the underlined focus words.

At the Shoe Store

X: I want some <u>shoes</u>.
Y: What <u>kind</u> of shoes?
X: The <u>beautiful</u> kind!
Y: <u>Black</u> or <u>brown</u>?
X: Neither. I'm <u>tired</u> of black and brown. I want <u>red</u> shoes. <u>Shiny</u> red shoes!

2 Underline the focus words in these dialogues. Practice making the focus clear.

1. *A Traveler*

X: Where are you going?
Y: Europe.
X: Where in Europe? To the north or to the south?
Y: Neither. I've seen the north and the south. I'm going east.

2. *Two People on the Street*

X: What are they building?
Y: They're building a school.
X: What kind of school? Elementary or high school?
Y: Neither. I think it's a trade school.

3. *Two Students*

X: What are you doing?
Y: I'm studying.
X: Studying what? Math or English?
Y: Neither. I'm sick of math and English. I'm studying nutrition, because I'm always hungry.

Note "Hungry" is the focus of the last part of the last sentence. But "always" could also be emphasized, if the speaker feels strongly. Do not emphasize too many words, however, because there will be less contrast and so the meaning will not be clear.

4. *A Tourist*

X: What's the best part of Canada?
Y: That depends. Do you prefer the city or the countryside?
X: Well, I like scenery.
Y: Then you should go to the far north of Canada.
X: Do they have good shopping there?
Y: Maybe you'd better go to Toronto.

E

Pair practice: disagreement

Practice these dialogues with your partner. Take turns saying the first remark. Emphasize the underlined word.

1. X: Dallas is in California
   Y: That's not right. It's in Texas.

2. X: I buy books at the library.
   Y: No, you buy books at the bookstore.

3. X: I buy books at the library.
   Y: No, you borrow books at the library.

4. X: A ship is smaller than a boat.
   Y: I don't think so. A ship is bigger than a boat.

5. X: You got home late!
   Y: Not <u>very</u> late.

6. X: You're always losing things!
   Y: Not <u>always</u>.

7. X: Florence is the capital of Italy.
   Y: No, <u>Rome</u> is.

8. X: "Actual" means "in the present time."
   Y: No, "actual" means "<u>real</u>."

F

Pair practice: dialogue 🔲

Underline the focus words and practice.

Two Students Argue

A: I bought some books at the library.
B: They don't sell books at the library. They lend books there. They sell books
   at the bookstore. Didn't you know that?
A: On Tuesdays they sell surplus books at the library.
B: Surplus?
A: Extra ones that they don't need.
B: I didn't know that.
A: There's a lot you don't know.

G

Pair practice: guessing what comes next

You can often guess what will come next by noticing which word the speaker has emphasized. Guessing what will come next is a good way to listen to English more effectively.

Student 1 says sentence (a) or (b). One way to make this exercise more fun is to hum the sentence (use "mmmmm" instead of words). Or you could use a kazoo (toy humming instrument). Student 2 listens closely to the pitch pattern and then says the answer, being careful to emphasize the focus word.

1. a. It's a big <u>dog</u>.   No, it's a wolf.
   b. It's a <u>big</u> dog.   More medium sized.

2. a. But we asked for two <u>Cokes</u>!   Oh, I thought you wanted tea.
   b. But we asked for <u>two</u> Cokes!   Oh, I thought you wanted one.

3. a. I heard that you bought a big <u>TV</u>.   No, it was a computer.

   b. I heard that you bought a <u>big</u> TV.   No, it was a little one.

4. a. He went by fast <u>train</u>.   Not by air?

   b. He went by <u>fast</u> train.   Not by the regular one?

5. a. I think that hamburger's <u>mine</u>.   No, this one is yours.

   b. I <u>think</u> that hamburger's mine.   Aren't you sure?

6. a. Is that a silver <u>watch</u>?   No, it's a bracelet.

   b. Is that a <u>silver</u> watch?   No, it's white gold.

7. a. We prefer beef <u>soup</u>.   Not stew?

   b. We prefer <u>beef</u> soup.   Not chicken?

8. a. Is there milk in the <u>refrigerator</u>?   No, on the table.

   b. Is there <u>milk</u> in the refrigerator?   No, but there's juice.

H

Disagreement

1 Write answers that disagree with the following statements. Different answers are possible.

2 Underline the word in your answer that disagrees with the statement.

3 Then practice with a partner.

Example A: London is far away.

          B: *No, it's <u>near</u>.*   or *Not very <u>far</u>.*   or *Not as far as <u>Rome</u>.*

1. A: Paris and London are countries.
   B: _____

2. A: Children learn to read before they learn to talk.
   B: _____

3. A: Old people can usually run faster than young people.
   B: _____

4. A: It isn't important to study hard in school.
   B: _____

5. A: Lemons are sweeter than honey.
   B: _____

6. A: China is a smaller country than Japan.
   B: _____

I
What was said?

Read Speaker B's statement. What did Speaker A say to cause an answer with this emphasis?

Example A: *Today is Monday.*

     or *Today is Wednesday.*

     B: No, today is Tuesday.

1. A: _____
   B: No, the wedding is on the fifth of April.

2. A: _____
   B: I don't agree. We need more rain.

3. A: _____
   B: But we prefer to keep the window open.

4. A: _____
   B: Blue is the best color for a car.

5. A: _____
   B: No, I think it's on page seven.

J
Summary: focus

At the beginning of a conversation, the focus is usually the last *content* word in a sentence. After the beginning, the focus can be *any* word.

The signals of focus:

- The *pitch rises* on the stressed syllable.
- The stressed syllable is very long.
- The stressed syllable is very clear.

K
Check yourself

1 Underline the focus words. Different people might choose different words.

2 The pronouns underlined in the dialogue("I" and "you") should be emphasized . Can you guess why the speaker emphasizes these words? Unit 14 will explain.

3 Record the dialogue.

4 Listen to check if you have emphasized the underlined words.

Food

X: Do you think food in this country is expensive?
Y: Not really.
X: Well, I think it's expensive.
Y: That's because you eat in restaurants.
X: Where do you eat?
Y: At home.
X: I didn't know you could cook.
Y: Well, actually I can't. I just eat bread and Coke.
X: That's awful!
Y: No, it isn't. I like bread and Coke.
X: You're crazy!

Review
Limerick: content words

Practice saying the limerick. If you reduce the schwa vowels and stress the important words, the rhythm will be exact.

I **knew** a **man** from **Ar**kansas*
Who **ate** a **rock** that **broke** his **jaw**.
    What do you **think**?
    He **said**, with a **wink**.
Per**haps** it's **wrong** to **eat** them **raw**.

*Pronounced "Arkansaw."
wink to close one eye, meaning "This is a joke."
raw uncooked
jaw the lower part of the mouth

14 Focus 2: emphasizing structure words

The normal emphasis pattern reduces structure words. However, when a speaker feels strongly or wants to disagree with something said before, *any* word may be emphasized, including structure words.

Example   A: Don't you agree that you should work harder?   (contracted)
     B: I do <u>not</u> agree!   (full form)

A
Pair practice: **and, or**

Take turns being Speaker A and Speaker B.

1. A: Our specialties are lamb, steak, and lobster.   (reduced)
   B: Terrific! I'll have steak <u>and</u> lobster!   (emphasized)

2. A: Which is more important – intelligence ør effort?
   B: Both – you need intelligence <u>and</u> effort.

3. A: Do you want pie ør cake?
   B: Neither. I don't like pie <u>or</u> cake.

4. A: Are you getting married for love ør money?
   B: What do you think? Love <u>and</u> money.

5. A: Are you going to go by plane ør train?
   B: Neither, I don't like planes <u>or</u> trains.

B
Pair practice: **can**

Take turns being Speaker A and Speaker B.

1. A: Do you think you cån do the job?   (reduced)
   B: Oh yes! I certainly <u>can</u> do it!   (emphasized)

2. A: He cån write well.
   B: I suppose he <u>can</u>. But he usually doesn't make the effort.

3. A: Cån we get this project done by Thursday?
   B: Of course we can, maybe even by <u>Wednesday</u>.

4. A: I don't think a country cán run out of money.
   B: Unfortunately, it can, if the government can't borrow.

5. A: This team cán win.
   B: Maybe it can, but I doubt it will.

C

Pair practice: not

Take turns being Speaker A and Speaker B.

1. A: Don't you think you should pay for dinner?   (contracted)
   B: No, I do not!   (emphasized)

2. A: Will you let them stay at your apartment?
   B: No, I will not!

3. A: It's cold.
   B: It's not cold.

4. A: Can't you loan me the money?
   B: No, I cannot.

5. A: Please try.
   B: No, I just cannot do it!

D

Pair practice: auxiliaries (is, have, had, would, will, are*)*

Take turns being Speaker A and Speaker B.

1. A: The train's already left.
   B: It has?   (shows surprise)

2. A: You should've answered right away.
   B: I did answer!   (shows strong disagreement)

3. A: I'd like a higher salary.
   B: Perhaps you would, but it isn't possible. (shows emphasis on wishing)

4. A: But the boy doesn't want to do it.
   B: Well, I say he will do it!   (shows strong feeling)

5. A: We're ready. Why aren't you?
   B: But we are ready!   (shows strong disagreement)

E

Pair practice: prepositions (in, on, over, up, etc.)

Take turns being Speaker A and Speaker B.

1. A: Is the cat on the bed again?
   B: No, she's under the bed.

2. A: You forgot to leave the keys on the desk again.
   B: I'm sorry, I put them in the desk!

3. A: I thought you wanted the lamp on the table.
   B: No, I said over the table.

4. A: Are the birds in the bird cage?
   B: Oh. I'm afraid I let them out.

5. A: If you're going out, please buy some film.
   B: Sorry, I'm coming in.

F

Pair practice: pronouns (I, you, me, we, they, etc.)

Take turns being Speaker A and Speaker B.

1. A: It seems cold.
   B: It doesn't seem cold to me.

2. A: Did you misplace your keys?
   B: No, I didn't. You were the one who had them last.

3. A: Do you like to argue with your friends?
   B: Not at all. But they like to argue with me.

4. A: People always forget to leave a tip.
   B: I don't forget!

5. A: Your team doesn't have a chance of winning!
   B: Well, we don't think so!

6. A: Hi! What's new?
   B: Nothing much. What's new with you?

7. A: This is a great party!
   B: I don't think it's a great party.
   A: But it is!
   B: No, you just want it to be.

G

Pair practice: pronouns that begin with H

Take turns being Speaker A and Speaker B.

1. A: Does she like classical music?
   B: No, but he does.
   ("he" is emphasized so the **H** is pronounced)

2. A: Did you or George make this terrible mess?
   B: Honestly, he did!

3. A: Is this the best you can do?
   B: Yes, but I think her work is even worse!

4. A: Where's Michael's English book?
   B: I don't know. Ask him about it.

5. A: Jerry showed me your fine report.
   B: It wasn't really mine – it's his work mostly.

H

Rhythm

Practice this poem. Do you understand why the underlined pronouns are emphasized?

Behold the hippopotamus!
We laugh at how he looks to us,
And yet in moments dark and grim
I wonder how we look to him.
Peace, peace, thou hippopotamus!
We really look all right to us,
As you no doubt delight the eye
Of other hippopotami.
                    (Ogden Nash)

I

Pair practice: what will come next?

1 Read the sentence and then write your own ending. Underline the word that should be emphasized (the focus word) in the part you wrote.

2 Dictate your sentences to your partner. Did your partner underline the focus word you emphasized?

1. We had a lot of rain last year, but _____.

2. I don't like to write, but _____.

3. This pen doesn't write very well, but _____.

4. Tomatoes are expensive, but _____.

5. My sister got a raise in pay, but _____.

J

Pair practice: checking information

In the following dialogues, Speaker Y emphasizes the question word ("how," "what," "why," etc.) to find out what Speaker X said.

X: Millie let the cat out!
Y: Who did?
X: Millie did.

X: I don't particularly like goat cheese.
Y: What kind of cheese?
X: Goat cheese.

This is a useful way to ask about something you did not understand or did not hear clearly.

Read each dialogue and write a question for Speaker Y. Then take turns reading the dialogue with correct emphasis.

1. X: We need tomatoes for the sauce.
   Y: _____
   X: Tomatoes.

2. X: John needs a new battery for his car.
   Y: _____
   X: John.

3. X: The travel agent made a mistake in our arrangements.
   Y: _____
   X: The travel agent.

4. X: Melissa is coming at five o'clock.
   Y: _____
   X: Five.

5. X: We went to the airport by bus.
   Y: _____
   X: To the airport.

6. X: Richard has a mountain of books on his desk.
   Y: _____
   X: On his desk.

7. X: They won't let you into the building without a badge.
   Y: _____
   X: A badge.

8. X: Mr. Johnson forgot to sign his name.
   Y: _____
   X: Mr. Johnson.

K

Pair practice: what was said?

When you are listening to a conversation, you may not hear all the words. You may need to guess what the person said. Think about the emphasis in B's remark and guess what A said before

Example   A: _She left at ten o'clock._   or   _She left at one o'clock._
          B: No, she left at eleven.

Write remarks for A. Then practice the dialogues.

1. A: _____
   B: I think it is _more_ important!

2. A: _____
   B: No, _you_ were the one who left the door open!

3. A: _____
   B: But we _have_ read our assignment!

4. A: _____
   B: No, we don't want to buy a TV _or_ a VCR!

5. A: _____
   B: The book for this class is _not_ expensive.

6. A:_____

    B: Well, you should be sorry!

7. A:_____

    B: But I do want to help you.

8. A:_____

    B: Unfortunately, the skunk was inside the house.

L

Pair practice: dialogue

1 Working alone, underline the focus words.

2 With your partner, take turns reading the dialogue out loud. Can you identify which words your partner chose to emphasize?

Remember, you do not have to agree on your choice of focus words, but you *do* have to make your choice clear.

New York Cab Driver

Driver: Where to?

Customer: The World Trade Center.

Driver: Where are you from?

Customer: Chicago.

Driver: Yeah, that's what I thought, from the accent.

Customer: Really? I have an accent? Funny, I never thought about it. Where are you from?

Driver: Atlanta, Georgia.

Customer: Really? You're from the South? You don't sound Southern.

Driver: No, of course not. I'm studying to be an actor and you can't have any accent if you want to be an actor.

Customer: So you just got rid of your Southern accent?

Driver: That's right. I wiped it out completely.

Customer: That's really interesting. I guess that's why you sound like you're from New York.

Driver: I do?

M

Small group discussion

1 Read the paragraph on page 101. Underline the focus words. A sentence may have more than one focus word, but if you underline too many, it will be hard for the listener to tell which words are important to you.

2 Take turns reading the sentences from the paragraph. The listeners should write the words they think you have chosen as the focus of each sentence.

3 Discuss your choice of focus. Not everybody will choose the same words.

Cultural Differences

[1]It is a lot of work to learn a new language. [2]When you work so hard to speak in that language, you certainly want to be understood. [3]But understanding is based on more than language. [4]Sometimes understanding is based not only on what you say but how you say it. [5]For example, every country has its own rules about politeness. [6]How do you thank someone? [7]How do you interrupt politely? [8]These rules are based not on language but on culture. [9]A polite style in one country may not seem like a polite style in a different country. [10]This can cause unexpected difficulties. [11]Therefore, when you learn a language it is useful to learn the rules of politeness as well. [12]Even if you think these rules are unnatural, using them can help you be understood better.

N

Half of a telephone conversation

1 Read what Speaker A says and underline the focus words.

2 Write B's half of the conversation and underline the focus words.

3 Read this conversation aloud with your partner. Then practice your partner's conversation.

    A: Hi! Did you hear the news?

    B: _____

    A: The news about our club?

    B: _____

    A: Our singing club.

    B: _____

    A: We've been invited to enter a national competition! We could be famous!

    B: _____

    A: Certainly we're ready to compete.

    B: _____

    A: Well I think so. We just need to spend a lot of time practicing.

    B: _____

    A: Fred, what's important – studying for your exams or helping us win the competition?

O
Pair work: writing a dialogue

1 Write a short argument between two speakers. Circle which words to emphasize.

2 Listen to your partner's dialogue. Write the emphasized words as you notice them. Did you guess which words your partner wanted you to notice?

3 Now read your dialogue aloud while your partner writes the emphasized words. Did your partner guess which words you had marked?

> The most important part of communication
> is to make it easy for your listener.

Review
L *and* R *sounds*

Practice saying this poem.

> How doth the little crocodile
>   Improve his shining tail,
> And pour the waters of the Nile
>   On every golden scale!
>
> How cheerfully he seems to grin!
>   How neatly spreads his claws,
> And welcomes little fishes in
>   With gently smiling jaws!
>   (Lewis Carroll)

doth old word for "does"
scale small bony flakes covering fish and reptiles

15 Intonation: pitch direction of questions

🔲 **Rule** A statement ends with a falling pitch. A question may end with a rising or a falling pitch.

The two most common types of questions in English are:

■ Questions that ask for information with a question word ("who," "when," "where," etc.).

1. X: Where are you going? ↘   Pitch falls
   Y: To Europe. ↘

2. X: What are you doing? ↘
   Y: I'm studying. ↘

3. X: What's new? ↘
   Y: Nothing much. ↘

■ Questions that can be answered "Yes" or "No."

1. X: Do you work in an office? ↗   Pitch rises
   Y: Yes, I do. ↘

2. X: Is it raining? ↗
   Y: Yes. ↘

3. X: Are there any good movies on TV tonight? ↗
   Y: No, there aren't. ↘

A

Pair practice: pitch patterns

1 Working alone, draw a pitch arrow at the end of each of these sentences.

2 Then practice these ten questions with a partner. Listen to each other's intonation.

Examples   Where do you work? ↘
              Do they pay well? ↗

1. Would you like another piece of cake? ↗
2. Can I give you some more coffee? ↗
3. When did you arrive here? ↘
4. Do you like it here? ↗
5. Are you married? ↗

6. What kind of work do you do? ⤵

7. Where did you grow up? ⤵

8. Do you have any sisters or brothers? ⤴

9. What are their names? ⤵

10. Do you think I ask too many questions? ⤴

B

Pair practice: dialogues

Draw pitch arrows at the end of each sentence. Then practice the dialogues.

1. ***Language Study***

A: Do you think English is easy?
B: No, I don't.
A: Why not?
B: I have to work too hard.

2. ***Cat Obedience***

A: Do you think cats can be trained?
B: Of course they can.
A: Really? I mean, can you train them to come when you call?
B: Certainly. Just put out food and call "Here, Kitty, Kitty, Kitty!"
A: Oh. And how can you train them to stay off the kitchen table?
B: That's easy. Just spray them with water whenever they jump up.
A: Does that mean I always have to be in the kitchen?
B: Well, I'll admit that is a problem.

C

Ways of checking information 📼

If you are not sure about what you just heard, there are two common ways to check the information:

- Checking information with a question word.
  The question word is the focus and the pitch rises. Listen and practice.

  1. X: Our computer isn't working.
     Y: What did you say? ⤴

  2. X: They got here at one o'clock.
     Y: When did they get here? ⤴

3. X: My in-laws are coming.
   Y: <u>Who</u> are coming? ➚

■ Checking information by repeating words.
  These words are actually part of complete yes/no questions, so the pitch rises.

1. X: We need twenty more plates.
   Y: Twenty? (Did you say twenty?) ➚

2. X: The party is on the fifth of May.
   Y: The fifth? (Is it on the fifth?) ➚

3. X: We have to finish the work before Tuesday.
   Y: <u>Before</u> Tuesday? (Not <u>after</u>?) ➚
   X: Yes, that's right.

D

Pair practice: questions that check information by repeating words

Draw a pitch arrow after B's question. Then practice the dialogues with a partner. Be careful to make the pitch of your voice follow the arrow.

Example A: John's coming.
           B: John's coming? ➚
           A: Yes.

1. A: He's coming for the party.
   B: The party?
   A: Yes, the office party.

2. A: How many people are coming?
   B: Forty.
   A: Forty?
   B: Yes.

3. A: How many people are coming?
   B: Forty.
   A: <u>How</u> many?
   B: Forty.

4. A: Where will the party be?
   B: At the Sailors' Club.
   A: The <u>Sailors'</u> Club?
   B: That's right.

E

Pair practice: what was said?

Read the dialogue and fill in the missing question. Then compare your answer with your partner. (You may have different answers.)

1. A: When does the show start?
   B: At 2:30.
   A: _____?
   B: That's right.

2. A: How much will it cost?
   B: Twenty dollars a person.
   A: _____?
   B: Twenty dollars.

3. A: How late will it last?
   B: At least until 10.
   A: _____?
   B: Yes.

4. A: What's the show about?
   B: The French Revolution.
   A: _____?
   B: Exactly.

F

Check yourself

Read the following dialogue and draw pitch arrows at the ends of sentences. Then record the dialogue and check to see if you followed the arrows.

Cones

(A host is taking a visitor for a drive in the mountains.)

Visitor: What kind of trees are those?
   Host: Pine trees.
Visitor: I see. Then are those things that are hanging from the trees pineapples?
   Host: No, apples grow on apple trees, but pineapples don't grow on pine trees. In fact, I don't think they grow on trees.

Visitor: What do they grow on?

Host: Some kind of bush. That's smaller than a tree.

Visitor: Oh. Well then, what do you call those things on the
pine trecs?

Host: Those are pine cones.

Visitor: Cones? Oh, I see . . . are they called "cones" because
they're shaped like ice cream cones?

Host: Exactly.

Review

Focus words

Underline the focus words. Then practice the dialogue with a partner.

A: Do you like books?

B: Sure. I read all the time.

A: What do you like best?

B: Serious books.

A: Serious about what?

B: Love.

A: Love isn't a serious topic.

B: It's a serious topic for me.

16 Intonation: thought groups (1)

[cassette] The English speaker helps to guide the listener by providing these "road signs":

- The focus word is emphasized.
- Words are grouped into thought groups.

A thought group is a group of words that belong together. There are two main signals to mark the end of a thought group: **pause** and **falling pitch**.

A pause gives listeners time to understand what was said. If people have trouble understanding you, making a pause at the end of a thought group can help them.

The pause must come at the right time, especially when you are saying numbers – in addresses, telephone numbers, and so on. When numbers are written, you can tell where the pause should be because of a space or punctuation (such as a hyphen or parentheses).

Listen to these two numbers:

    (a) 5551314
    (b) 555-1314

Did you hear the difference?

Practice saying this North American phone number: (415) 555-1212.

Area code	Local code	Personal number
415	555	1212

A

Pair practice: telephone numbers

1 Student 1 dictates (a) or (b). Student 2 writes what he or she hears. Was the grouping correct?

    1. a. 4163 254 324
       b. 416 325 4324

    2. a. 40 841 34567
       b. 408 413 4567

    3. a. 201 32 54636
       b. 201 325 4636

2 Now dictate your own telephone number. Did your partner write it with the correct grouping?

B

Change of pitch 📼

Every thought group has a focus word. The focus word is marked by a rise and then a fall. The fall in pitch helps the listener to recognize the end of a thought group.

Listen and practice.

1. I work for the United Nations.

2. I remembered to bring paper, but I forgot my book.

C

Pair practice: arithmetic

1 Student 1 says either (a) or (b) with a pitch fall at the end of each group. The new group starts on a higher pitch. This shows the listener the beginning and ending of the group. Student 2 says the answer. The correct answer depends on correct grouping.

📼 *Examples* $(2 + 3) \times 5 = 25$
two plus three times five equals twenty-five

$2 + (3 \times 5) = 17$
two plus three times five equals seventeen

1. a. $3 \times (3 + 5) = 24$
   b. $(3 \times 3) + 5 = 14$

2. a. $(5 - 2) \times 2 = 6$ (five minus two)
   b. $5 - (2 \times 2) = 1$

3. a. $(4 - 1) \times 3 = 9$
   b. $4 - (1 \times 3) = 1$

4. a. $(10 - 1) \times 2 = 18$
   b. $10 - (1 \times 2) = 8$

5. a. $(4 + 2) \times 3 = 18$
   b. $4 + (2 \times 3) = 10$

6. a. $(2 \times 2) + 3 = 7$
   b. $2 \times (2 + 3) = 10$

2 Now invent your own problem:

7. a. _____
    b. _____

D

Either/or questions 🔲

Either/or questions offer a choice. Both choices are focus words, so they get equal emphasis.

Examples   Would you like black or brown?
             Are you going east or west?

Practice asking these questions.

1. Do you want to work or rest?
2. Are they good or bad?
3. Is the ring silver or gold?
4. Will you go by bus or train?
5. Do you want soup or salad?

E

Pair practice: a series of items 🔲

Rule 1   The pitch pattern shows which items belong in the series.

Rule 2   The final item in a series has the rise-fall that means "the end."

   Examples   USAID (U.S. Agency for International Development)
                We want soup, salad, coffee, and pie.

Practice these thought groups, paying attention to pitch patterns.

1. PR (public relations)
2. WHO (World Health Organization)
3. red, blue, and green
4. We need books, pencils, and paper.
5. They sell Fords, Mazdas, and BMWs.
6. We have a computer, a fax, and a modem.
7. red, blue, green, and yellow
8. The zoo has elephants, tigers, bears, and lions.
9. The students come from France, Japan, Malaysia, and Argentina.
10. His suitcase contains socks, underwear, ties, pajamas, shirts, and a sweater.

F

Adding to the series: alphabet game

Students take turns adding an item to the list. Each new item begins with the next letter of the alphabet. (Remember to have a rise and fall in pitch on the last item.)

Example   **I'm Going to New York**

First Player: I'm going to New York and I'm taking an **apple**.
Second Player: I'm going to New York and I'm taking an apple and a **bicycle**.
Third Player: I'm going to New York and I'm taking an apple, a bicycle , and a **cap**.
Fourth Player: I'm going to New York and I'm taking an apple, a bicycle, a cap, and a [something that begins with the letter "d"].

A player who cannot remember the whole list is out of the game and the next player continues and adds an item.

G

Check yourself

1 Underline the focus words and mark a slash (/) at the end of each thought group.

2 Then practice the dialogue with a partner. Be careful to make the thought groups clear. Each thought group must have a focus word.

Difficult Children

Mother: We want a turkey and cheese sandwich; an avocado, lettuce, and tomato sandwich; and a peanut butter and jelly sandwich.
Waitress: On white, whole wheat, or rye?
Mother: The turkey and cheese on rye, and the other two on whole wheat.
First Child: No! No! I want white bread!
Mother: Whole wheat is good for you.
Second Child: I don't want avocado, lettuce, and tomato!
Mother: OK, one turkey and cheese on rye and two peanut butter and jellies on white.
Waitress: What would you like to drink?
Mother: One Diet Pepsi and two glasses of milk.
First Child: We want Pepsi!
Mother: OK, OK. Three sandwiches, one Diet Pepsi, and two regular Pepsis.

H
Summary

> To help your listener understand:
>
> - Emphasize the focus words.
> - Use pauses or pitch falls at the end of thought groups.
> - Use long pauses at the end of complicated ideas.

Review
Linking

Practice saying these common expressions as one word (no pause in between parts of the group).

1. Hurry up!
2. How are you?
3. How's it going?
4. What's new?
5. Hi there!
6. How do you do?
7. No problem!
8. See you later!

Review
Content words

The first poem is traditional. The second is having fun with it.

Circle the content words in each poem. Then say the poems.

Twinkle, Twinkle – Twice

1. Twinkle, twinkle, little star,
   How I wonder what you are!
   Up above the world so high,
   Like a diamond in the sky.
   > (Jane Taylor)

2. Twinkle, twinkle, little bat,
   How I wonder where you're at!
   Up above the world so high,
   Like a tea tray in the sky.
   > (Lewis Carroll)

17 Intonation: thought groups (2)

A
Review

The last content word in a thought group usually has the focus emphasis. There is a rise on the stressed syllable of that word and then a fall. This change in pitch marks the focus of the thought group.

Examples a. John said, "The boss is crazy."   Who is speaking?
           b. "John," said the boss, "is crazy."   Who is speaking?

B
Pair practice: sentences

Student 1 says either sentence (a) or (b) and then asks the question that follows. Student 2 answers the question.

1. a. Alfred said, "That clerk is incompetent!"   Alfred
    b. "Alfred," said that clerk, "is incompetent!"   that clerk
      Question Who was speaking?

2. a. The teacher said, "That student is lazy."   the teacher
    b. "The teacher," said that student, "is lazy."   that student
      Question Who was speaking?

3. a. "Jack believes," I said, "that he's sick."   that he's sick
    b. Jack believes I said that he's sick.   that I said that he's sick
      Question What does Jack believe?

4. a. He sold his house, boat, and car.   three
    b. He sold his houseboat and car.   two
      Question How many things did he sell?

5. a. She likes pie and apples.   pie and apples
    b. She likes pineapples.   pineapples
      Question What does she like?

6. a. Do you want Super Salad?   one
    b. Do you want soup or salad?   two
      Question How many things were you
              offered?

7. a. Did she choose a greener blue?   one
    b. Did she choose a green or blue?   two
      Question How many colors were there?

8. a. Wooden matches are used to start fires.   one
    b. Wood and matches are used to start fires.   two
    Question How many sorts of things are used to start fires?

9. a. The store sells golden jewelry.   one
    b. The store sells gold and jewelry.   two
    Question How many types of things does the store sell?

10. a. When the water boils rapidly, put the spaghetti in the pot.   when the water boils rapidly
    b. When the water boils, rapidly put the spaghetti in the pot.   when the water boils
    Question When should you put the spaghetti in the pot?

C

Pair practice: story

It is helpful to pause after a complicated idea so that the listener has time to understand what was said. There should also be a pause after "road sign" words like:

however	nevertheless	first of all
finally	furthermore	on the other hand

These words help the listener to follow the meaning. Emphasis and pause make ideas easier to notice.

1 Underline the focus words in the following story. There are many focus words because the speaker is upset.

2 Mark good places to pause.

3 Take turns listening to each other saying the story. Did you use emphasis and pauses to help the listener follow the story?

A Sad Story

[1]This was the most terrible day of my life! [2]Everything went wrong. [3]First of all, I couldn't find my keys. [4]Then I knew I was going to be late for work, so I drove too fast and got a speeding ticket. [5]When the officer asked for my driver's license, I realized that I had left it at home! [6]I got a flat tire and had to change it, which took even more time. [7]Finally, when I arrived at work, I remembered that it was a holiday and the office was closed!

D
Poem

This is the most famous nonsense poem in English. Do not worry about pronouncing the nonsense words – just hum the poem. Can you guess how to make the pauses and pitch patterns?

Jabberwocky

'Twas brillig, and the slithy toves
Did gyre and gimble in the wabe;
All mimsy were the borogoves,
And the mome raths outgrabe.

(Lewis Carroll)

E
Small group work

1 Read this paragraph silently. Mark places where you think a pause should be made to give the listener time to think.

2 Take turns reading two or three sentences to your group. They should make a small mark to show where you paused.

3 Check to see if the other students could tell where you paused.

4 Discuss the reasons why each student chose to pause in a particular place.

Cultural Differences

[1]In your country, is it considered polite to listen quietly to other people, without any change of expression on the face? [2]If this is the style you have learned, perhaps you should watch two North Americans talking. [3]Notice how the person who is listening will have frequent changes of expression. [4]The listener may also make short remarks while the other person is talking. [5]These may be one word, like "Really?" or they may just be a sound, like "uh-huh" or "mmmm." [6]This is how North American listeners show that they are listening in a friendly way. [7]That is why North Americans get uneasy when the listener is completely silent and shows no change of expression. [8]In the American style of conversation, an unmoving face often means that the listener is unfriendly, or perhaps even angry.

F

Check yourself: dialogue

If possible, record this with your partner. Were the separate items and groups made clear?

Coffee Shop Confusion

(The customer doesn't hear very well, and the waiter is impatient.)

Customer: What can I have to start with?
Waiter: Soup or salad.
Customer: What's Super Salad?
Waiter: What do you mean "Super Salad"?
Customer: I thought you just said you have a Super Salad.
Waiter: No, we don't have anything like that. Just plain green salad. And tomato soup.
Customer: Oh, OK. Well, what do you have for dessert?
Waiter: We have pie and apples.
Customer: I don't care much for pineapples.
Waiter: Are you making jokes or what? We have pie and apples.
Customer: OK, OK. Just give me the soup and a piece of apple pie.
Waiter: Sorry, the only pie we have is berry.
Customer: Very what?
Waiter: What?
Customer: You said the pie was very something. Very good?
Waiter: Mmmm, I said the pie was berry. And if you will wait just a minute, I'm going to get another waiter to serve you.

Review

Focus words: the meaning of emphasis

What is in the speaker's mind?

Student 1 says sentence (a) or (b). Student 2 says the most likely meaning of that sentence.

1. a. We want three tickets for today's show. (not two)
   b. We want three tickets for today's show. (not tomorrow's show)

2. b. Please give me both books.   (Both of them are important.)
   a. Please give me both books.   (I really want them.)

3. a. Gary used to be sensible.   (He didn't do dumb things.)
   b. Gary used to be sensible.   (He isn't sensible now.)

4. a. Speak to her again.   (She might listen.)
   b. Speak to her again.   (Maybe a second time will work.)

5. a. They should have stayed later. (They left too early.)
   b. They should have stayed later. (It would have been better.)

6. a. I didn't know she was out there. (I thought she was inside.)
   b. I didn't know she was out there. (I thought it was just him.)

7. a. I think I paid $5 for just one box. (I'm not sure.)
   b. I think I paid $5 for just one box. (Maybe it was two boxes.)

8. a. I told you about that.   (I didn't tell anyone else.)
   b. I told you about that.   (Perhaps you weren't listening.)

Appendix A
Vowels

Below are the three English vowels that are the farthest apart in the mouth. They form three points of a triangle. Close your eyes and try them silently, sliding your tongue back and forth to the three farthest points of the triangle.

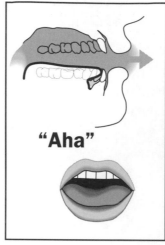
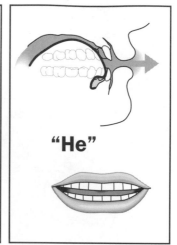

Note To make a true English "who" vowel, the lips must be rounded. To make a true English "he" vowel, the lips must be smiling.

Below is a triangle showing the English vowels.

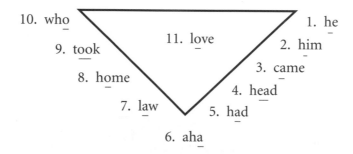

10. who
9. took
8. home
7. law
6. aha
11. love
5. had
4. head
3. came
2. him
1. he

A

Vowels 1, 6, and 10 (he, aha, who)

Listen to the following words and think about how the tongue, lips, and jaw move. Then practice saying the words.

he .... who   (tongue moves backward)
he .... aha   (tongue and jaw move down)
aha .... who   (tongue and jaw move up)
who .... he   (tongue moves forward)

118

B

Vowels 1–10 contrasted with vowel 11

Vowel 11 is the central vowel and is the most common vowel sound in English. This sound is used for words like "love," but it is also used for the unstressed vowel schwa. It is used for schwa because it is the closest position for the tongue to get to from any other place in the mouth.

Listen to the contrast between vowel 11 and all the other vowels.

1.	beat	11.	but
2.	bit		but
3.	bait		but
4.	bet		but
5.	bat		but
6.	bot (as in "bottle")		but
7.	bought		but
8.	boat		but
9.	book		buck
10.	boot		but

C

Listening for vowel 11

Listen to the following repetitions of a word. One word is different in each set of words. The different word has vowel 11, as in "but" and "love." Mark a check for the word with that vowel.

	A	B	C

Example You hear: leak   leak   luck

You check: ✓

A	B	C		A	B	C
1.			6.			
2.			7.			
3.			8.			
4.			9.			
5.			10.			

D

Listening for vowels 1 and 2 (he *and* him)

Listen to the following repetitions of a word. One word is different in each set of words. Mark a check for the one that is different.

	A	B	C
1.			
2.			
3.			
4.			
5.			

	A	B	C
6.			
7.			
8.			
9.			
10.			

E

Saying words with vowels 1 and 2 (he *and* him)

The following pairs of words are identical except for the vowel sounds. Practice making a clear contrast between the two vowels.

Vowel 1 (he)	Vowel 2 (him)	
feet	fit	*2 1 2 1*
eat	it	Is he busy?
seen	sin	
teen	tin	*2 1 1*
steal	still	busy bee
seat	sit	

F

Pair practice: sentences with vowels 1 and 2

Student 1 says sentence (a) or (b). Student 2 answers.

1. a. Why did you sleep?   I was tired.
   b. Why did you slip?   The floor was wet.

2. a. What's a sheep used for?   Wool.
   b. What's a ship used for?   To carry things on the water.

3. a. When will you leave?   Tomorrow.
   b. When will you live?   I'm living now!

4. a. How do you spell "leap"?   L E A P
   b. How do you spell "lip"?   L I P

5. a. What does "beat" mean?   To hit.
   b. What does "bit" mean?   The past tense of "bite."

G

Spelling for vowels 1 and 2

Practice saying these two vowel sounds. These vowels can be spelled in different ways.

1 "he"	2 "him"
clean	gift
teach	picnic
reach	nickel
bean	little
speak	Britain
needle	symbol
seem	syllable
keep	myth
thief	busy
belief	pretty
ceiling	

H

Pair practice: dialogue

1 In the dialogue on page 122, put a "1" over the vowels that sound like "he" and a "2" over the vowels that sound like "him." The number of these vowels appears in parentheses at the end of the line.

2 Practice reading the dialogue aloud with another student. Be careful with these vowels.

Big Brother and Little Sister

Sister:	Billy, Billy, teach me to read!	(7)
Brother:	You're too little.	(1)
Sister:	No I'm not. I'm <u>big</u>! <u>Very</u> big!	(3)
Brother:	I'm busy. Here's a nickel for some candy.	(4)
Sister:	A nickel? That's too little! I need fifty cents.	(5)
Brother:	Hmmm. It would be cheaper to teach you to read!	(5)

I

Review of vowel 11 (love)

Listen to the following groups of words. Mark a check for the word that is different.

A	B	C		A	B	C
1.				5.		
2.				6.		
3.				7.		
4.				8.		

J

Pair practice: review of vowel 11 in sentences

Student 1 says sentence (a) or (b). Student 2 answers.

1. a. Is it a big cat?   No, it's a lion.
   b. Is it a big cut?   No, not too deep.

2. a. What's a buck?   One dollar.
   b. What's a book?   The thing you're reading.

3. a. Was it cut?   No, it was broken.
   b. Was it caught?   No, it's still free.

4. a. What's a skull?   The bone that protects your brain.
   b. What's a school?   A place for learning.

5. a. Do you need many?   No, just a few.
   b. Do you need money?   Yes, ten dollars.

6. a. What's a goal?   An aim or purpose.
   b. What's a gull?   A sea bird.

K

Listening for vowels 3 and 8 (**came** _and_ **home**)

Listen to the following groups of words. Mark a check for the one that is different.

	A	B	C
1.			
2.			
3.			
4.			
5.			
6.			

L

Pair practice: vowels 3, 7, and 8 (**came, law, home**)

Student 1 says sentence (a) or (b). Student 2 answers.

1. a. What's paper for?   To write with.
   b. What's pepper for?   Flavor.

2. a. What's a coat?   A long jacket.
   b. What's a cat?   An animal.

3. a. What's a pawn?   A chess piece.
   b. What's a pun?   A play on words.

4. a. How do you spell "lane"?   L A N E
   b. How do you spell "lawn"?   L A W N

5. a. What's on the bone?   Meat.
   b. What's on the bun?   Butter.

6. a. What's "waste" mean?   Something you throw away.
   b. What's "west" mean?   The opposite of east.

7. a. What does "fame" mean? Celebrity.
   b. What does "foam" mean? Lots of bubbles.

8. a. Where's the lake?   In the mountains.
   b. Where's the lock?   In the door.

9. a. When do you pause?   When I'm finished.
   b. When do you pose?   When I'm having my picture taken.

10. a. What does "cost" mean? The price.
    b. What does "coast" mean? Land along the ocean.

Appendix B
Additional work on consonants

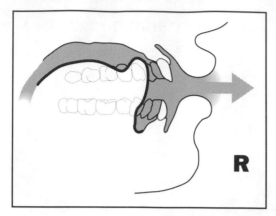 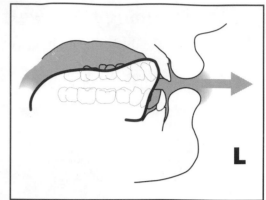

Do not touch the roof of the mouth for **R**. Touch the tooth ridge for **L**.

Note The lips are rounded for **R**.

A
R *and* L

Practice saying the following words with a partner. Choose a word and ask, "Which column?"

1	2	3
ray	lay	day
row	low	dough
reap	leap	deep
red	led	dead
room	loom	doom
rye	lie	die

B
Linking: R *and* L

1 Link the final sound slowly, concentrating on the tongue position at the time of linking.

1. all around   all over   sell ice   will ever   all ages
    our age   hear it   far away   for every   fear enemies

2. sell everything   tell Annie   We'll all agree.
    call all active   call after

3. tear out   far away   fear our enemies
    car or airplane   for each   Where are all our able enemies?

2 Make a new word by linking.

1. He will owe a lot of money.   will owe.....low

    Is it high or low?

2. What is their age?   their age.....rage

    Great anger is "rage."

C

Pair practice: R *and* L

Student 1 says sentence (a) or (b). Student 2 answers.

1. a. Is it right?   No, it's wrong.
    b. Is it light?   No, it's dark.

2. a. What's a lamb?   A baby sheep.
    b. What's a ram?   A male sheep.

3. a. Where's the load?   In the truck.
    b. Where's the road?   Through the valley.

4. a. How do you spell "rain"?   R A I N
    b. How do you spell "lane"?   L A N E

5. a. How do you spell "irrigation"? I R R I G A T I O N
    b. How do you spell "allegation"? A L L E G A T I O N

D

G *and* W

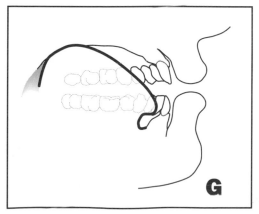
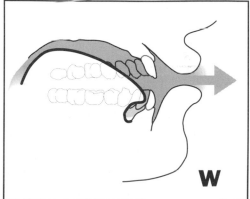

Practice saying these words.

1	2
gate	wait
get	wet
go	woe
guide	wide
good	wood

E

Pair practice: **G** *and* **W**

Student 1 says sentence (a) or (b). Student 2 answers.

1. a. What does "guile" mean?   Trickery.
   b. What does "while" mean?   During.

2. a. How do you spell "gate"?   G A T E
   b. How do you spell "wait"?   W A I T

3. a. What does "go" mean?   The opposite of "come."
   b. What does "woe" mean?   Sadness and sorrow.

4. a. What's a "wage"?   Salary.
   b. What's a "gauge"?   A measuring device.

5. a. What does "guide" mean?   To lead.
   b. What does "wide" mean?   The opposite of "narrow."

6. a. Is that good?   No, it's bad.
   b. Is that wood?   No, it's plastic.

F

Consonant clusters

Many languages do not allow consonants to be said together, but English has many of these "consonant clusters." If you practice linking these sounds, it will be easier for you to say the clusters at the end of words.

1. "ks"   so / make so / We make so many.   makes
2. "nd"   doll / plan doll / He planned all the work.   planned
3. "zd"   door / close door / Leave it closed or open.   closed
4. "ld"   Dan / call Dan / He called Dan.   called
5. "vz"   zoo / save zoo / Save zoo animals.   saves
6. "rd"   Dave / cure Dave / The doctor cured Dave.   cured

G

Additional practice: Z and S

Student 1 says sentence (a) or (b). Student 2 answers.

1. a. He raised a horse.   Where did he keep it?
   b. He raced a horse.   Did it win?

2. a. Did you like the place?   Yes, it was beautiful.
   b. Did you like the plays?   Yes, they were funny.

3. a. You need to sip slowly.   Why, is it hot?
   b. You need to zip slowly.   Why, is the zipper broken?

4. a. He's interested in the prizes.   Does he expect to win?
   b. He's interested in the prices.   Does he plan to buy?

5. a. What's a president?   The elected leader.
   b. What's a precedent?   The first time for something.

6. a. What does "lazy" mean?   Not energetic.
   b. What does "lacy" mean?   Made of lace.

7. a. What does "easy" mean?   The opposite of "hard."
   b. What does "EC" mean?   The European Community.

8. a. What's fussy?   A crying baby.
   b. What's fuzzy?   A toy rabbit.

H

Additional practice: stops

Practice saying these words.

| Beginning sound | | Final sound | |
Voiced	Unvoiced	Voiced	Unvoiced
bay	pay	tab	tap
do	to	seed	seat
game	came	bag	back

| Middle Sound | |
Voiced	Unvoiced
tabbing	tapping
wedding	wetting
bagging	backing

I

TH/T(unvoiced) and TH/D(voiced)

Practice the voicing contrast with continuants and stops.

	Continuants	Stops
Voiced	they	day
	than	Dan
	those	doze
	loathe	load
Unvoiced	thought	taught
	thank	tank
	thin	tin
	theme	team
	bath	bat

J

Pair practice: TH/D, TH/T, P/B

Student 1 says sentence (a) or (b). Student 2 answers.

1. a. What does "their" mean?   Something belongs to them.
   b. What does "dare" mean?   To challenge someone.

   v
2. a. How do you spell "though"?   T H O U G H
   b. How do you spell "dough"?   D O U G H

   uv
3. a. Is it a good theme?   Yes, a fine topic.
   b. Is it a good team?   No, they never win.

   v
4. a. What does "then" mean?   At that time.
   b. What does "den" mean?   A house for a fox.

   uv
5. a. Was it thin?   No, it was fat.
   b. Was it tin?   No, it was silver.

6. a. "No parking."   That's for cars.
   b. "No barking."   That's for dogs.

7. a. Did they bring a pair?   Yes, two.
   b. Did they bring a bear?   Yes, it was enormous!

K

Pair practice: **TH/S** *(unvoiced) and* **TH/Z** *(voiced)*

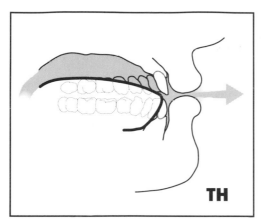
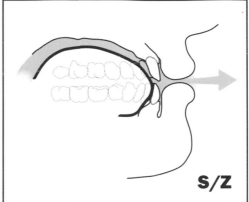

Student 1 says a word from list A or list B. Student 2 says "one" or "two," depending on which word he or she hears.

Example Student 1: miss
              Student 2: two

Unvoiced				Voiced	
1	2	1	2	1	2
myth	miss	Beth	Bess	teethe	tease
bath	buss	youth	use (noun)	soothe	Sue's
path	pass	faith	face	lathe	laze
math	mass				

L

Pair practice: **F** *and* **P**

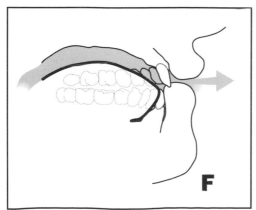
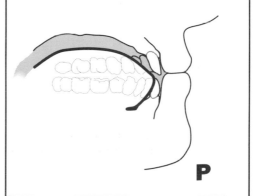

Student 1 says a word from list 1 or list 2. Student 2 says "one" or "two."

Beginning Sound		Final Sound	
1	**2**	**1**	**2**
fat	pat	laugh	lap
fail	pail	wife	wipe
foot	put	cliff	clip
face	pace		
feet	Pete		

M
Pair practice: sentences

Student 1 says sentence (a) or (b). Student 2 answers.

1. a. What does "fast" mean?   Quick.
    b. What does "past" mean?   Something is finished.

2. a. What's a fool?   A stupid person.
    b. What's a pool?   A place to swim.

3. a. What does "fair" mean?   Something like "equal."
    b. What does "pair" mean?   Two of the same kind.

4. a. What's a foal?   A baby horse.
    b. What's a pole?   A long stick.

5. a. How do you spell "wife"?   W I F E
    b. How do you spell "wipe"?   W I P E

6. a. How do you spell "lab"?   L A B
    b. How do you spell "laugh"?   L A U G H

7. a. The copy machine doesn't work.   Go to the copy shop.
    b. The coffee machine doesn't work.   Go to the cafe.

Review
Stops and continuants: additional practice

Practice saying these words.

Beginning sounds		Middle sounds		Final sounds	
pan	fan	ladder	lather	soup	Sue
ban	van	leaping	leafing	boat	bowl
chair	share	washing	watching	bite	buy
tank	thank			road	rose
lock	dock			mate	main
face	pace				

Review
Pair practice

Student 1 says sentence (a) or (b). Student 2 answers.

1. a. How do you spell "3"?   T H R E E
   b. How do you spell "tree"?   T R E E

2. a. What's a bath for?   To get clean.
   b. What's a bat for?   To play ball.

3. a. How do you spell "witch"?   W I T C H
   b. How do you spell "wish"?   W I S H

4. a. What does "suit" mean?   A set of clothes.
   b. What does "soothe" mean?   To calm someone.

5. a. What does "leap" mean?   To jump.
   b. What does "leaf" mean?   Part of a plant.

6. a. What's a mitt?   A sock for your hand.
   b. What's a myth?   A magic story.

7. a. Do you like soup?   Only tomato.
   b. Do you like Sue?   Yes, she's nice.

8. a. What are you watching?   A movie.
   b. What are you washing?   The dishes.

9. a. What does "line" mean?   Something like "good."
   b. What does "pine" mean?   A kind of tree.

10. a. What does "thought" mean?   The past tense of "think."
    b. What does "taught" mean?   The past tense of "teach."

11. a. What's the date?   June first.
    b. What's the rate?   Twenty percent.

12. a. Is it dead?   No, it's alive.
    b. Is it red?   No, it's orange.

13. a. What's a dam?   A wall to hold water.
    b. What's a lamb?   A baby sheep.

14. a. What's a ship?   It's a boat.
    b. What's a chip?   It's a small piece.

15. a. Where's the boat?   On the water.
    b. Where's the vote?   On the paper.

16. a. What's a van?   A kind of truck.
    b. What's a ban?   A prohibition.

Appendix C
Student's own dictation

A
Dictation

1 Choose two long sentences from your own work or field of study. Write any technical terms that may be unfamiliar to the class on the board.

2 Dictate the sentences to the class. If possible, make a recording while you dictate.

3 Have two or more students write on the board as you dictate while the rest of the class writes on paper. When students cannot guess a word, they should leave a blank in the sentence.

4 Now write the two sentences on the board so that the class can see what you dictated.

5 With the help of the teacher, analyze as a class the errors and misunderstandings.

B
Analysis

Compare the speaker's version and the listeners' versions. Missing or faulty words may be a **listener** error. However, when two or more listeners have misunderstood the same word, it is a sharp indication that the speaker must correct some error in his or her speech.

1 *Identify the content words.* Mistakes with content words (nouns, main verbs, etc.) cause more confusion than mistakes with structure words (articles, prepositions, etc.). For instance, when a listener mistakes a noun for a verb it becomes very difficult for the listener to predict what kinds of words are coming next.

2 *Circle the focus words.* A long sentence is apt to have several thought groups, and each group will have a focus. A missed focus word will cause confusion of the thought.

3 *Check the stressed syllables of focus words.* Was the stress on the right syllable? Were the sounds accurate? A substitution of the wrong sound in these syllables is serious.

C
Conclusion

Have the class practice saying the sentences with you so that everybody understands and can apply the analysis. Then re-record the sentences and compare as a class the two versions on tape.